T0182335

VIRUS HUNTERS

**HOW SCIENCE PROTECTS PEOPLE WHEN
OUTBREAKS AND PANDEMICS STRIKE**

Also by Amy Cherrix

*In the Shadow of the Moon: America, Russia,
and the Hidden History of the Space Race*

*Eye of the Storm: NASA, Drones, and the Race
to Crack the Hurricane Code* (Scientists in the Field)

*Backyard Bears: Conservation, Habitat Changes,
and the Rise of Urban Wildlife* (Scientists in the Field)

VIRUS HUNTERS

HOW SCIENCE PROTECTS PEOPLE WHEN OUTBREAKS AND PANDEMICS STRIKE

AMY CHERRIX

HARPER

An Imprint of HarperCollinsPublishers

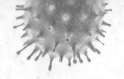

Library of Congress Control Number: 2023944828
ISBN 978-0-06-306954-1

Typography by Michelle Gengaro-Kokmen
24 25 26 27 28 LBC 5 4 3 2 1
First Edition

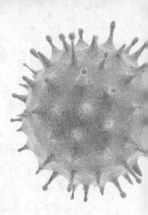

This book is dedicated to public health professionals, past and present,
who guard the boundary between people and pandemics.

Contents

Prologue

When you picture a detective, what image comes to mind? Is it a fast-talking private eye interrogating a suspect in a windowless room? Or the fictional nineteenth-century detective Sherlock Holmes, trudging through London's rain-soaked streets in his long coat and iconic deerstalker hat with a magnifying glass held close to his eye, scouring crime scenes for clues to catch a killer?

But what if the suspect wasn't a person? What if the threat was a microscopic menace—a dangerous virus or bacterium capable of infecting human beings and making them sick? What kind of detective does it take to nab a biological assassin that's invisible to the naked eye?

The answer is a disease detective! Known as epidemiologists, these scientists study how diseases and disorders emerge and spread in a population of people. In Atlanta, Georgia, the Centers for Disease Control and Prevention (CDC) is home to one of the world's most elite squads of epidemiologists: the Epidemic Intelligence Service. The EIS officers describe their work as "shoe-leather epidemiology," which is exemplified by the EIS logo: the sole of a shoe with a hole worn through it, superimposed over the globe. The symbol emphasizes the connection between epidemiologists and the old-school detectives who traveled by foot, interviewing witnesses while trying to solve a mystery or stop a killer—think Sherlock Holmes with a microscope in place of a magnifying glass! EIS officers rely on the same basic detective skills to track down the source of an outbreak. Working closely with members of affected communities, they interview witnesses and gather clues to identify the cause of illness, locate those who are sick—or who could become sick—and uncover the source of the outbreak, in an effort to halt it in its tracks. And they do not work alone. There are other public health professionals who help to guard the boundary between people and pandemics: virologists (those who study viruses), vaccinologists (who develop vaccines), and immunologists (who study the immune system).

Perhaps the most recognizable immunologist in recent memory is Dr. Anthony Fauci. As director of the National Institute of Allergy and Infectious Diseases (NIAID) for thirty-eight years, the physician-scientist advised seven US presidents on issues of public health, and was known as "America's Doctor." During the COVID-19 pandemic, Dr.

Fauci became a household name because he was a frequent presence in the media. But that's not the case for most public health professionals, whose crucial work takes place behind the scenes. As a general rule, these service-minded people pursue careers in public health because they want to be part of something larger than themselves. For that reason, they rarely seek the spotlight. Nevertheless, humankind owes them an immense debt. *Virus Hunters* brings you some of their courageous—and hopeful—stories.

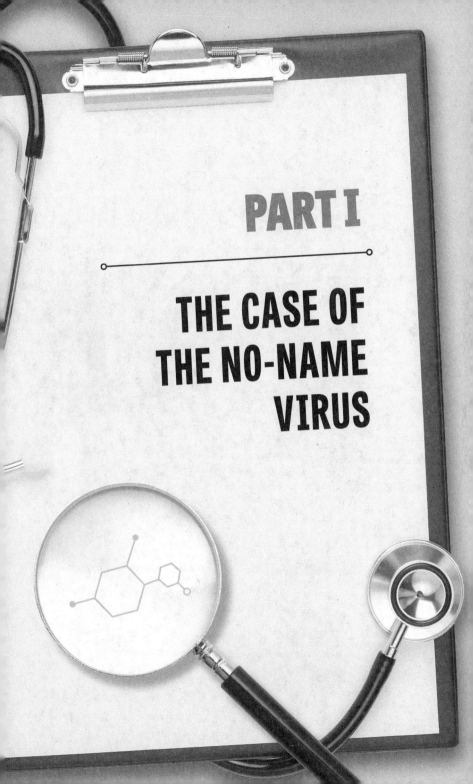

PART I

THE CASE OF THE NO-NAME VIRUS

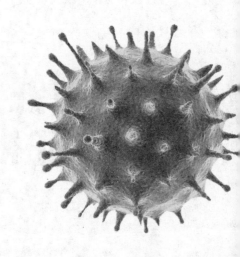
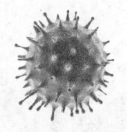

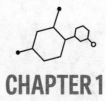

CHAPTER 1

The Epidemic Intelligence Service

Friday, May 28, 1993

A freight train was heading for Jay Butler. He rolled his bicycle to a stop, keeping a safe distance from the tracks at the Frazier Road rail crossing. Butler was pedaling from his home in Tucker, Georgia, to his office in Atlanta. Later that afternoon, his wife and kids would pick him up from work and the family would travel to North Carolina for the long Memorial Day weekend. But for now, Butler was stuck, with no choice but to wait while the train inched down the track. He was going to be late for work.

Dr. Jay Butler was a physician at the Centers for Disease Control and Prevention. Founded in 1946 as the Communicable Disease Center to control the spread of malaria in the US, its role gradually expanded to include other public health threats: chronic illnesses, like diabetes and heart disease;

Dr. Jay Butler still works for the CDC, where he serves as the deputy director of infectious diseases at the agency.

and social problems, such as violence, poverty, and racism. But the CDC is best known as the agency that investigates and responds when dangerous pathogens, both known and unknown, emerge and make people sick.

Butler was a recent graduate of the CDC's Epidemic Intelligence Service, the two-year intensive program that has trained medical professionals in epidemiology since it was founded in 1951. During their training, EIS officers are deployed to investigate outbreaks in the US and around the world.

When Butler finally arrived at the CDC that morning in late May of 1993, he quickly stowed his bike, then hurried toward his office. A colleague stopped him and asked

Butler to attend a meeting with Jim Hughes, director of the National Center for Infectious Diseases. For almost two weeks, the CDC had been following the outbreak of a mysterious respiratory illness in New Mexico. If local and state health officials were unable to contain it, the CDC was prepared to help. But as an agency of the federal government, it could not offer assistance to any state until a formal request was received. According to Hughes, the state of New Mexico's call for help had just come through. That's when Jay Butler's weekend plans began to fall apart.

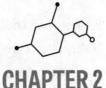

CHAPTER 2

The Index Cases

Two weeks earlier
Friday, May 14, 1993
Gallup Indian Medical Center
Gallup, New Mexico

Nineteen-year-old Merrill Bahe was the picture of health—a former high school track star and nationally recognized athlete. But none of that fit what Dr. Bruce Tempest, chief of internal medicine, and the emergency room staff at the Gallup Indian Medical Center observed when Bahe arrived by ambulance. He was suffering from severe pulmonary edema, a condition that causes an excess buildup of fluid in the lungs. Doctors and nurses raced to save Bahe's life, doing everything in their power to revive him. But they were unsuccessful. The loving young father and gifted athlete died. The ER team was baffled. No one understood what could have caused sudden respiratory failure in an otherwise healthy young man. Bahe's cause of death was a medical mystery.

By New Mexico state law, the Office of the Medical Investigator (OMI) must be notified about any deaths from unknown causes. The day Merrill Bahe died, Deputy Medical Investigator Richard Malone was on duty at OMI. After taking the call from the Gallup Indian Medical Center, he went straight to the hospital to open an investigation. Malone consulted with Dr. Tempest, who described

High school track star Merrill Bahe loved to run through New Mexico's scenic backcountry.

the sudden severity of Bahe's unexplained respiratory illness and the horrible condition of his lungs, which were completely saturated in fluid. It triggered a memory for Malone, as he recalled a similar case from the previous month at this same hospital. He had investigated the death of a young woman who had also died of an unexplained respiratory illness. Like Merrill Bahe, she, too, was a resident of the Navajo Nation. The deputy director of OMI, Dr. Patricia McFeeley, had performed an autopsy but had been unable to determine the etiology, or cause of death. Malone telephoned her to discuss Bahe's case. McFeeley told Malone that she also thought the two deaths might be connected and agreed to perform an autopsy on Bahe.

Malone believed it was vital to find out what had caused Bahe's sudden death, especially if it could be related to the earlier case he and McFeeley had investigated. But before the autopsy could take place, Malone had to approach Merrill Bahe's grieving loved ones in the hospital and ask them for permission to release his body. It was a difficult question to ask of anyone, but for the Diné (Navajo), death is a taboo subject.

Malone met with the family and gently explained that an autopsy was necessary because the doctors did not know what had caused Bahe's untimely death. Whatever had made him sick, he said, could be contagious. To Malone's relief, the family granted consent for the autopsy. But as the conversation continued, Malone learned that Bahe's twenty-one-year-old fiancée, Florena Woody, had also recently died. In fact, her funeral was taking place that day.

Florena Woody and Merrill Bahe had been high school sweethearts. After graduation, Bahe enrolled at Navajo Technical University, where he studied architectural drafting. The couple shared a home in the small town of Littlewater, thirteen miles east of Crownpoint, New Mexico, which was part of the 27,000-square-mile Navajo Reservation. Bahe and Woody had recently welcomed their first child, five-month-old Maurice, and were engaged to be married.

But in early May, their happy life began to unravel. Florena Woody got sick, complaining of flu-like symptoms, body aches, and a fever. By May 8, her health had not improved, and she went to see a doctor at Crownpoint Healthcare Facility. Her blood work did not reveal any reason for concern, but Woody was asthmatic, so out of an abundance of caution, the doctor admitted her.

The next day, chest X-rays showed her lungs were filling with fluid. As the hours passed, it grew more difficult for her to catch her breath, and every cough produced a white foamy liquid, signaling that her respiratory system was failing. By the time a helicopter could be arranged to take her to a bigger hospital in Albuquerque, Florena Woody had died. Merrill Bahe was devastated. The love of his life was gone, leaving him to raise their child alone.

Through a haze of grief, Bahe began preparing for Woody's funeral. At some point, he, too, began to feel sick.

After two days, Bahe could no longer ignore his flu-like symptoms and went to see a doctor at Crownpoint Healthcare Facility. The physician knew about the recent death of his fiancée from similar, but more severe, symptoms. He conferred with another doctor. They agreed that Bahe didn't have to be admitted to the hospital but warned that he should immediately return if his symptoms worsened. Bahe left the hospital with medication for the flu and pneumonia. The doctors who treated him had no way of confirming that Merrill Bahe was sick with a life-threatening illness that would eventually kill him.

By May 14, the morning of Florena Woody's funeral, Bahe's health had declined even further. He needed to go to the hospital but refused to return to Crownpoint, where Woody had died. Instead he wanted to go to another hospital, the Gallup Indian Medical Center. It was an hour away in Gallup, New Mexico, the same town where Woody's funeral would take place that day. Woody's cousin Karoline agreed to drive Bahe to the hospital. During the trip, his condition continued to deteriorate. Thirty miles outside Gallup, Karoline wheeled into a convenience store parking lot to call 911. Before the ambulance could arrive, Bahe collapsed.

As Richard Malone listened to the story of how Florena Woody and Merrill Bahe had died, three things became clear. First, there was a strong likelihood that Bahe and Woody had died of the same mysterious illness. Second, OMI had not known about Woody's case until that day because she had died at Crownpoint, an Indian Health Service hospital on the Navajo Reservation. The Navajo Nation is governed by tribal law, not New Mexico state law, so the reservation clinic was not required to report her death to Malone's office. Third, if these cases were evidence of a previously unknown illness, it could have been circulating unnoticed for a while. Bahe and Woody could be the index cases—the patients first identified by public health officials in an outbreak. If so, others living on the reservation could have been exposed. There could be more unreported cases, and more deaths.

Malone rushed from the hospital to Florena Woody's funeral to ask her family to authorize an autopsy as well.

Dr. Patricia McFeeley began the autopsies on Merrill Bahe and Florena Woody that night. The first test was for *Yersinia pestis*, the type of bacteria that causes bubonic plague, a disease responsible for some of the worst pandemics in world history. Plague is a zoonotic disease, meaning it is an infection that can spread from animals to people. From 1347 to 1351, the plague devastated Europe during a pandemic known as the Black Death. Twenty-five million people died. Today, plague is no longer a pandemic illness because it's treatable with antibiotics. However, cases continue to pop up around the world. Plague can be fatal if the infection isn't caught in time, especially in countries where access to lifesaving medications is limited or nonexistent.

Every year, between one and seventeen people are diagnosed with plague in the US. In the desert southwest, fleas that live on a prairie dog can carry *Yersinia pestis* in their gut. A prairie dog contracts plague from fleas when the infected insects draw their blood meal from its body. Plague is most often spread to humans through the bite of an infected flea.

Both Bahe's and Woody's tests for plague were negative, as were the tests for other possible causes of death: influenza, Legionnaires' disease, and anthrax. McFeeley was at a loss. She found nothing to explain why the young couple's lungs were so saturated with fluid, weighing twice as much as healthy lungs. "Why aren't we smart enough to figure this out?" she recalled asking herself at the time. With both autopsies proving inconclusive, state health officials alerted the CDC to the emerging outbreak. As the investigation on the ground in New Mexico intensified, America's disease detective agency monitored the situation from Atlanta.

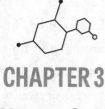

CHAPTER 3

A House Call

Dr. James Cheek was a physician, epidemiologist, and former EIS officer who, at the time of the hantavirus outbreak, worked with the Indian Health Service in Albuquerque. The IHS is the federal agency that provides health services to the nearly 3 million American Indians and Alaska Natives who belong to 574 federally recognized tribes in thirty-seven states. As an enrolled member of the Cherokee Nation of Oklahoma, Cheek was proud of his work with the IHS. "The agency provides a much-needed service to tribal communities that are often left behind by our public health system," he said.

Cheek was dispatched to the home of Merrill Bahe and Florena Woody to search for evidence to explain the couple's sudden illness. Chemical poisoning was one possibility. But

Cheek didn't find evidence of chemical contaminants in or around the house, just an abundance of mouse droppings under the sink in the kitchen. He wasn't surprised. The mice were everywhere that spring. Heavy rains the previous winter had resulted in a bumper crop of pine nuts from the region's piñon trees. With the abundance of available food, the mouse population was booming. Cheek's investigation, however, like McFeeley's autopsy, proved inconclusive.

By May 20, ten suspected cases had been reported. Four days later, in response to the worsening outbreak, the New Mexico Department of Health sent a notice to every physician in the Four Corners region (New Mexico, Colorado, Utah, Arizona). It described the severe and possibly viral respiratory illness and noted its high mortality rate of 75 percent. Two days later, the number of suspected cases had nearly doubled. And by May 27, at least eight people were dead. There were confirmed cases in New Mexico and Arizona, with others under investigation in Texas. The letter urged doctors to report any current or past cases matching the description, and the public was advised to avoid close contact with anyone who exhibited symptoms of flu.

The release of the letter heightened media coverage of the outbreak, and the mystery illness striking the Four Corners region soon became national news.

CHAPTER 4

An Epidemic of Misinformation

The panic that gripped the Four Corners region sparked another outbreak: renewed racism against Indigenous people. The media spread misinformation that stigmatized Diné (Navajo). *USA Today*—a national newspaper—ran the headline: NAVAJO FLU CLAIMS 11, suggesting the illness was somehow exclusive to people of the Navajo Nation. But not every person who contracted the mystery illness was Native American.

The media, hungry for stories at any cost, converged on Littlewater, shamelessly violating the privacy of the grieving Diné community. Without regard for their pain, or deference to their cultural beliefs about death and grief, reporters followed mourners, brazenly assaulting them with personal questions. For the Diné and other Indigenous people in the land now known as the United States of America, the shameful disregard for Native lives, sovereignty, and suffering was all too familiar.

One of the most brutal atrocities committed against the Diné was the Long Walk. During the mid-1800s they, and the Ndé (Mescalero Apache), endured repeated assaults from the US Army, who intended to destroy them and their way of life, and steal their land. Beginning in 1863, the Ndé and Diné were forced from their homes in a series of violent raids. At gunpoint, the army marched them 470 miles to Fort Sumner in the land now known as eastern New Mexico. Their destination, writes Roxanne Dunbar-Ortiz, was a "military concentration camp at Bosque Redondo," where at least 8,500 Diné and 500 Ndé were imprisoned. Many of those who managed to survive the brutality of the Long Walk perished there.

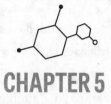

CHAPTER 5
Answering the Call

Friday, May 28, 1993

Back at the CDC's National Center for Infectious Diseases, director Jim Hughes chose Jay Butler as the senior staff person to lead the investigation in New Mexico. Butler immediately selected two EIS officers to accompany him, Dr. Jeffrey Duchin and Dr. Ron Moolenaar. Before the team departed Atlanta, they were issued a special piece of equipment—a respirator. The full-face mask would filter the air they breathed, protecting them from any airborne pathogens. But first the devices had to be tested. One by one, Butler, Duchin, and Moolenaar put on their masks and stepped into a smoke-filled room to check them for leaks. It was a sobering moment as the experts responding to the health crisis were reminded that they were risking their lives. If the outbreak was indeed airborne, and their masks failed, they could be exposed to the mysterious and possibly fatal disease they were trying to stop.

Later that night, as Butler packed for the trip, his eight-year-old daughter asked him how he would stay safe and healthy while he was protecting others. Butler reassured her that he would take all the necessary precautions, wearing personal protective equipment (PPE), including a mask and gloves.

Despite his reassurances, Butler knew that hunting down a killer pathogen was risky work. He and his team were headed for a "hot zone," an area with a high risk of contamination or infection. There was always a chance that he might not return. But Jay Butler loved his job and was thrilled for the chance to lead the CDC team. "There's this sense of going about your work, and then suddenly, there's an emergency call," he told journalist Steve Sternberg. "There's this sudden reordering of priorities, and you're on an airplane watching the skyline of Atlanta shrink behind you."

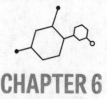

CHAPTER 6

"The Mystery Illness"

Saturday, May 29, 1993

The next morning, Butler, Duchin, and Moolenaar arrived at the University of New Mexico in Albuquerque for a weekend of meetings. They were part of an outbreak task force that included forty local and state health officials.

The first task was to establish a case definition for the syndrome at the heart of the outbreak, what doctors had been referring to as "The Mystery Illness" (or TMI). A good case definition contains the most basic information that medical professionals need to accurately diagnose an illness in a patient. TMI's case definition read: "a very simple severe case of pulmonary illness characterized consistent with acute respiratory distress syndrome occurring in a resident of New Mexico, Arizona, Utah, or Colorado, since January 1, 1993."

Going forward, every doctor in the Four Corners area would use this case definition to determine if a patient with similar symptoms could have TMI.

During the meeting, the group examined the records of possible cases reported since the death of Merrill Bahe. They brainstormed potential causes of the outbreak—including those previously ruled out by autopsies (plague, flu, Legionnaires' disease, herbicides, poison gases, rare fevers), wrote them on sheets of paper, and taped them to the walls of the conference room. As they studied case files, the investigators realized that those who survived The Mystery Illness recovered quickly, and that so far no one had contracted the disease in a clinical setting like a hospital. That was important—and encouraging—data because it suggested that TMI was not a highly contagious disease, capable of spreading between people. Infectious diseases that can be passed from person to person sometimes cause pandemics— widespread outbreaks over a large geographic area, like a country, or in some cases the entire world. As dangerous as the new outbreak was, at least it did not have the potential to ignite a pandemic.

By Monday, the task force had settled on three possible causes of The Mystery Illness. The first was a new and virulent type of influenza. The second was an environmental source—like exposure to an unregulated chemical. The third possibility was the most intriguing and challenging for the disease detectives: TMI could be caused by a previously unknown pathogen. If so, it could take weeks or even months to identify the source of the outbreak, develop treatment options, or find a cure. Until then, every day that passed without knowing the cause of TMI could cost more lives.

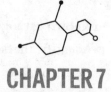

CHAPTER 7

Gathering the Evidence

Tuesday, June 1, 1993

After the weekend of meetings, the CDC team began their investigation. Jay Butler learned that state health officials expected him to not only coordinate the outbreak response between New Mexico and CDC headquarters in Atlanta but also be the face of the investigation. It was an unusual role for someone in Butler's position. Normally the job of CDC disease detectives is anonymous. They are public health scientists, not television personalities. Nevertheless, he stepped before the cameras and answered questions from the press, reassuring the public that the CDC was working closely with state and local health officials to find the source of the outbreak and stop it as soon as possible.

Meanwhile, EIS officer Jeffrey Duchin began a detailed medical record review of those who had become sick with

TMI, tracking the disease's progress on paper. Charts and X-rays told the story of the outbreak from a clinical perspective. The first signs were body aches, cough, and sometimes an upset stomach and dizziness. As the illness progressed, white blood cell counts rose, a signal that the body was fighting a foreign invader. As the capillaries of the lungs began to leak fluid, the organs became sodden, making breathing impossible. In chest X-rays of fatal TMI cases, the flooded organs could appear as a near whiteout. Death usually occurred within ten days of the onset of illness. In the chilling black-and-white X-ray images, Duchin saw the same tragic scenario play out over and over again.

While Duchin reviewed the case files, EIS officer Ron Moolenaar gathered the physical evidence. He boxed up tissue samples taken from the bodies of the sick and shipped them to the CDC's Viral Special Pathogens Branch (VSPB). The Atlanta-based squad of world-class infectious disease experts would use the samples to conduct their own unique brand of medical detective work. Like a molecular police lineup, they would compare samples taken from TMI victims against stock samples of twenty-five deadly pathogens in their laboratory, hoping to find a match and identify the killer.

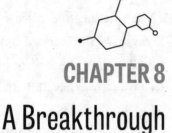

CHAPTER 8

A Breakthrough

Thursday, June 3, 1993

Two days later, inside a VSPB laboratory, a technician noticed that a blood sample from a New Mexico patient with The Mystery Illness was reacting with one of their stock samples. It was hantavirus, a virus that caused a disease known as hemorrhagic fever with renal syndrome. HFRS impairs the blood's ability to clot, which leads to hemorrhaging (bleeding) inside the body. Eventually the kidneys begin to fail. For the lab tech, the reaction raised more questions than it answered. If the Four Corners outbreak was hantavirus, why did it attack the lungs instead of the kidneys? Also, hantavirus had never been detected in the United States.

In 1951, however, it had sickened soldiers who were exposed to the virus during the Korean War. In June of that year, some American troops fighting in Korea came down with an unknown flu-like illness. The symptoms included a high fever, vomiting, and horrific aches in the body. In the worst cases, the kidneys failed, and the sick began to bleed uncontrollably when the hemorrhagic fever overwhelmed their immune system. As many as 121 service members died. The deadly outbreak alarmed the CDC leadership at the time, who suspected they had been the victims of a biological attack. In response, Dr. Joseph W. Mountin, founder of the CDC, decided that the United States needed an epidemic intelligence service.

Alexander Langmuir, the CDC's first chief epidemiologist, agreed with Mountin. He believed that gathering data through disease surveillance was vital to the protection of public health. To contain an outbreak, epidemiologists needed to know who was sick and how the illness was spreading. By regularly analyzing the number of cases and deaths caused by a disease, and sharing that information with other health workers, public health systems could be better prepared to address outbreaks.

Mountin tapped Langmuir to create an elite corps of epidemiologists at the CDC who would respond to public health threats, traveling wherever they were called to serve at a moment's notice. In July 1951, twenty-two physicians and one sanitary engineer became the first class of Epidemic Intelligence Service officers at the CDC.

Now, more than four decades later, a sample of hantavirus from the Korean War era appeared to be related to TMI. If The Mystery Illness was hantavirus, investigators had just found their first major clue: hantavirus was carried by rodents.

In the years following the Korean War, a mouse, *Apodemus agraius*, was discovered to be hantavirus's carrier. The rodent inhabited the Hantan River region of Korea, for which the virus was named. The United States military didn't realize it in the 1950s, but transmission of the virus had occurred when the dried urine and feces of infected mice was disturbed by the soldiers' activity. The disturbances released the pathogenic particles into the air, where they could be inhaled, sickening the troops.

When Jay Butler learned that TMI appeared to be hantavirus, he called a press conference to update the public. In the meantime, a microbiologist at the CDC in Atlanta prepared another test that would confirm the identity of The Mystery Illness.

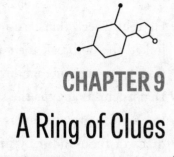

CHAPTER 9

A Ring of Clues

When Jim Cheek learned that TMI could be hantavirus, he shuddered, recalling the large quantity of rodent droppings he had found underneath the kitchen sink inside Merrill Bahe and Florena Woody's home. If TMI *was* hantavirus, he had risked his life when he entered the abandoned home without wearing any PPE, including a mask. But Cheek was a scientist. He had been using the most recent data available at the time to make decisions about safety. "At that point," he said, "we didn't have any inkling that there could be an airborne respiratory disease. We felt confident that we were not going to be exposed."

While he waited for confirmation that TMI was hantavirus, Cheek received an unusual phone call from a dendrochronologist at the University of Arizona in Tucson.

He told Cheek that he'd heard the news that the CDC had linked the outbreak to rodents and that he had some additional information that might be relevant to the investigation. Dendrochronology is the study of tree rings. Each year of a tree's life, a growth ring is created. A tree can live to be hundreds or thousands of years old. When dendrochronologists compare the growth rings of trees, they can read them like a history book about the tree's environment. Cheek was confused. How could the rings of a tree hold clues to an outbreak of disease?

The researcher explained that he had previously conducted a study of trees near the Zuni Pueblo in Tucson, Arizona. The trees' rings revealed alternating wet and dry years. While talking with A:shiwi (Zuni) people in the area, the dendrochronologist learned that there were more deaths during wet years than in dry years. That was odd, he thought. During wet years, the land would have been lush and fertile, and food more abundant. So why were *more* people dying? he asked. They told him that during wetter years, there were more mice, which led to a belief that the deaths were somehow related to the rising mouse population. Pueblo residents had learned to avoid mice, taking care to protect their grain stores from rodents. The tree researcher had been puzzling over this piece of data. When he heard about the possible connection between rodents and TMI, he realized the information could be relevant to the outbreak investigation.

Although "the story had come out of the blue," Cheek said, "everything sort of clicked." He agreed that the information was significant. It described an undeniable connection between the climate, the rising mouse population, and the higher rate of mortality observed by the Zuni. Health officials asked residents of the Navajo Nation about the information they'd received from the Zuni and learned that they, too, had noticed a rise in deaths following wet winters. "When you're doing an [outbreak] investigation," Cheek said, "you never know where information is going to come from."

The Diné and Zuni had appreciated and understood the close connection between climate, ecology, and outbreaks even before diseases could be identified with cutting-edge technology; before researchers learned to read climate changes in the rings of trees. Now scientists were playing catch-up. They were just discovering a disease that had been known to Indigenous people for generations.

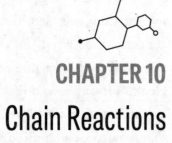

CHAPTER 10
Chain Reactions

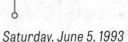

Saturday, June 5, 1993

At the CDC, microbiologists prepared to conduct a test that would confirm whether TMI was hantavirus. It was called polymerase chain reaction, or PCR. The same year that TMI emerged in New Mexico, biochemist Kary Mullis was awarded the Nobel Prize in chemistry for inventing the technology. Think of the PCR as a molecular photocopier that can amplify a segment of genetic material (DNA or RNA). In hantaviruses, that genetic material is RNA. The CDC scientists would use a PCR machine called a thermocycler to quickly create millions (or billions) of copies of a specific segment of the virus's RNA. All those copies would make it easier to view the virus's unique genetic sequence, which could then be compared to the genetic sequences of other viruses.

The CDC had been on the case for just eight days when the agency's microbiologists in Atlanta unmasked the Four Corners killer. The PCR test confirmed that not only was The Mystery Illness caused by rodent-borne hantavirus, it was a *different* type of hantavirus, one that attacked the lungs, not the kidneys. Scientists could finally give TMI a proper scientific name. They called it hantavirus pulmonary syndrome, or HPS.

How PCR Changed the World

During the COVID-19 pandemic, PCR has been considered the gold standard in testing for the virus. The technology has also been used to study the DNA of ancient animals, accurately identify criminals by the DNA left behind at a crime scene, and map the human genome!

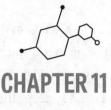

CHAPTER 11

The Cold Case

Thursday, June 10, 1993

Soon after the CDC confirmed its discovery of another hantavirus previously unknown to science, the agency prepared to publish a report of its findings in the *Morbidity and Mortality Weekly Report*. Known as the "voice of the CDC," the *MMWR* is the agency's weekly scientific digest for medical professionals. The report was being reviewed before its publication by the editor of the *MMWR*, former Epidemic Intelligence Service officer Rick Goodman. During his first deployment with EIS in 1978, Goodman had investigated an outbreak of an unusual respiratory illness in the midwestern US. The index case had been a young man who died in the hospital from severe pulmonary edema, leaving behind a wife and two small children. The autopsy proved inconclusive. But Goodman, who was haunted by the memory of the mysterious death, had kept in touch with the man's widow and saved his medical file.

As he read the article about the hantavirus discovery, he realized there was something eerily familiar about the cases. Goodman located the fifteen-year-old medical file and reviewed it once again. Suddenly everything about the cold case made perfect sense.

Goodman contacted the widow of the man who'd died and arranged to have a sample of his stored tissue released to the CDC for testing. The results confirmed the cause of death was hantavirus pulmonary syndrome. At last, Goodman could tell the man's family what had killed their loved one and lay his cold case to rest.

CHAPTER 12
Setting the Trap

The New Mexico outbreak investigation was moving quickly, but there was no cure for hantaviruses. The next step in saving lives was to stop transmission of the virus to keep more people from getting sick. To do that, the disease detectives needed to zero in on its source: the rodents that carried the deadly pathogen.

The CDC reached out to epidemiologist James "Jamie" Childs, one of the world's leading experts on hantavirus. Childs packed his bags and rodent traps and headed for New Mexico, where he began a two-month rodent-trapping operation. Teams from the CDC, Indian Health Service, and Navajo Nation's health department set hundreds of traps on Navajo land. It was dusty, hot, dangerous work. While setting the traps, team members decided not to wear PPE like masks and gowns. They did not want to risk frightening or further alienating residents of the Navajo Nation, whose lives and culture had already been disrupted by the outbreak. The trapping teams only wore PPE while processing the animals to obtain blood and tissue samples.

The trapping teams collected and tested approximately 1,700 individual rodents for hantavirus. Among them was *Peromyscus maniculatus*, also known as the deer mouse. Any artist hoping to draw an adorable picture of a mouse should consider *P. maniculatus* as their model. The tiny rodent's fur is soft grayish-brown in color. It has an impressive set of whiskers, comically oversized ears, big beady eyes, and a curious gaze.

After testing almost 2,000 rodents, the CDC's Viral

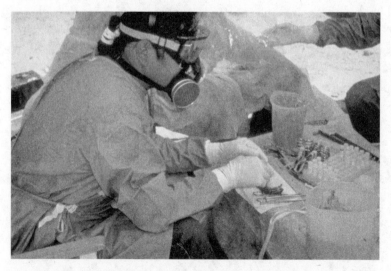

Dressed in head-to-toe PPE, disease detectives test rodents and other animals for hantavirus during the 1993 Four Corners outbreak.

Special Pathogens Branch reported that the picture-perfect mouse was the hantavirus's most frequent disease host. The mice had been infecting people in the Four Corners area with the deadly hantavirus contained in its saliva, urine, and feces. "The bad news," Childs said, "is that the deer mouse is probably the most widely distributed and populous of any rodents found in the United States." *Peromyscus*'s habitat ranges as far north as Alaska and Canada and south to central Mexico, excluding the southeastern US.

With this confirmation, residents and tourists in the Four Corners region were advised to keep their homes and cabins free of rodents by sealing any holes and placing mousetraps around dwellings. The CDC partnered with local and state health officials to educate the public about how to safely clean areas with evidence of rodent activity to prevent infection. Any person cleaning infested areas was urged to wear gloves

Even the most adorable of creatures is capable of carrying diseases that can make people sick. Never approach or disturb wild animals.

as well as a mask to prevent accidental exposure. Nests and droppings had to be soaked for five minutes with a mixture of bleach and water before removal.

As knowledge of the new virus circulated, along with advice for the safe removal of nests and droppings, case numbers plummeted. In late summer of 1993, the fatality rate from hantavirus pulmonary syndrome fell from 80 to 50 percent. By December, HPS cases were almost nonexistent. In all, thirty-one people contracted hantavirus in the 1993 outbreak and eleven died.

As the dust settled on the outbreak, another controversy arose. No one could agree on what to call the newly discovered hantavirus. The CDC suggested two possible names: Four Corners virus or Muertos Canyon virus. The Navajo Nation and the National Park Service rejected both names because they unfairly stigmatized those places, as well as the people who call them home. In the end, the mysterious virus that proved so difficult to name was called Sin Nombre, the "no-name" virus.

CHAPTER 13

Hantavirus Today

Since the CDC first began surveillance for the hantavirus in 1993, there have been fewer than a thousand cases of hantavirus pulmonary syndrome in the US. But there is still no known cure for hantavirus pulmonary syndrome. The best chance of survival is early diagnosis and quality intensive care at a hospital. For many people, however, including some of those who live on the Navajo Reservation, that kind of treatment can be too expensive and difficult to access in remote areas.

The 1993 Four Corners hantavirus outbreak illustrated the close relationship between human health and animal health. When abundant food supplies caused a spike in the mouse population, it increased the chances of people coming into contact with the hantavirus carried by the deer mice. It is a cautionary tale for the twenty-first century, as human intervention and climate change continue to alter the natural world, driving some animals, like rodents, from their habitats, forcing them to adapt to life closer to people. To stop the next pandemic before it starts, human beings must also become better stewards of the planet and its natural resources.

The CDC's disease detectives were able to solve the 1993 hantavirus outbreak in record time, thanks to the methods and tools of epidemiology. But who was the first person to identify those methods and tools and use them to track an outbreak within a population of people? The origins of disease detective work can be traced back more than 150 years to London, England. It was there that John Snow, a devoted doctor, took it upon himself to find the source of a deadly cholera outbreak. In the process, Snow would develop fundamental methods of investigation used in the science of epidemiology.

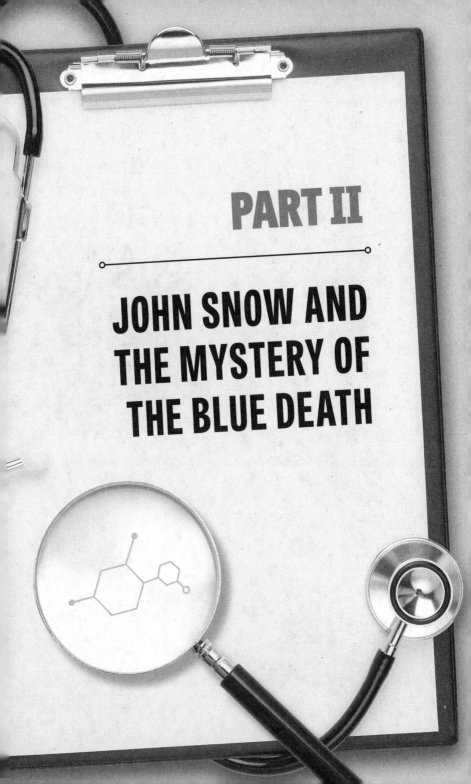

PART II

JOHN SNOW AND THE MYSTERY OF THE BLUE DEATH

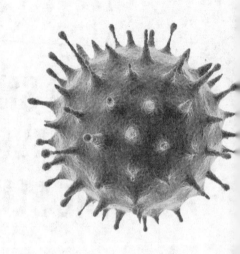

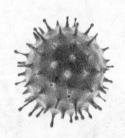

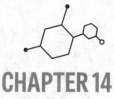

CHAPTER 14

The First Disease Detective

August 1854
London, England

Throughout his medical career, forty-one-year-old Dr. John Snow had confronted cholera more times than he cared to count. This time, the dreaded disease had come to Broad Street in Golden Square, a neighborhood in the Soho district of London, not far from Snow's home. During the first hours of the outbreak, seventy people had died. By the next day, cases numbered in the hundreds. There was no

Dr. John Snow, March 15, 1813–June 16, 1858, the world's first disease detective.

treatment for cholera at the time, and many people did not survive. A person could be healthy at breakfast and dead by dinnertime. At most, they lingered a few days.

The first sign of cholera is excruciating pain in the abdomen, followed by vomiting and then diarrhea that causes the body to lose water by the liter. Severe dehydration can cause blood pressure to drop so low that organs are robbed of essential oxygen, resulting in discoloration of the skin, a ghostly bluish tinge that is cholera's calling card. Eventually the body's organ systems fail, causing death.

Cholera Pandemics in World History

The Golden Square outbreak in the summer of 1854 took place during the world's third cholera pandemic. It's believed to have started in India in 1846. Emerging technology of the Industrial Revolution, like the steam-powered ship, was expanding world trade, and in the process expanding the reach of deadly diseases. Imperialism contributed to cholera's spread, as wealthy and powerful European nations like Britain grew their empires through colonization. Warfare and the migration of people around the world also fueled cholera outbreaks. According to the World Health Organization (WHO), the world is currently in the midst of its seventh cholera pandemic. This ongoing global outbreak is believed to have started in South Asia in 1961, spread to Africa in 1971, and to the Americas in 1991.

One of Snow's first experiences as a doctor in training had been to assist a local physician during a cholera outbreak among coal miners. As he cared for the ailing workers, Snow noticed their unsanitary working conditions. The miners labored eight to nine hours without returning to the surface, eating their meals and relieving themselves in the mine. "The pit is one huge privy," a coal mining community member told Snow, "and of course the men always take their [meals] with unwashed hands." Witnessing these conditions, the young doctor began to form an original theory about the cause of the disease. By 1849, Snow suspected cholera was transmitted to people by accidentally ingesting the feces of a person already sick with cholera, most likely through drinking contaminated water.

DEATH'S DISPENSARY.
OPEN TO THE POOR, GRATIS, BY PERMISSION OF THE PARISH

An artist's illustration depicts "Death" dispensing water tainted with cholera.

Snow also observed that the crowded living conditions of impoverished people made them more vulnerable to the disease. "It is amongst the poor, where a whole family live, sleep, cook, eat, and wash in a single room, that cholera has been found to spread when once introduced," he said. In these overcrowded homes, there was not enough space to isolate sick patients from the healthy members of the family, or to designate separate areas for food preparation. If the person who cared for the sick also cooked the meals and failed to properly wash their hands, they could accidentally transmit cholera to every person at the dinner table.

Snow noted that although members of the privileged class also frequently died of the disease, in "the better kind of houses . . . [cholera] hardly ever spreads from one member of the family to another." He concluded that hygiene was more convenient for the upper classes because they lived in spacious homes with access to plenty of water and towels for handwashing.

CHAPTER 15

The Miasma Theory

Snow's theory that cholera was a waterborne illness was a daring idea in the 1800s. Most doctors of the day believed that cholera was the product of a "miasma," an invisible cloud of illness that drifted up from decaying matter and floated through the air, making people sick. Miasma theory sounds absurd in the twenty-first century because we know now that disease is caused by microscopic viruses and bacteria. But for most nineteenth-century doctors, "bad air" was the only reasonable explanation for the outbreaks, especially given the filthy conditions of London in the mid-1850s.

London was bursting at its borders, the largest and most densely populated city in the world. Almost 3 million citizens—and their livestock—were squeezed into an area of less than 100 square miles. Try to picture yourself in the city during this time, 170 years ago, before public works infra-structure like sewage systems and water treatment plants were common. To wash, drink, or prepare food, your water had to be collected from one of the city's many public street pumps. Imagine the sights and smells you would have experi-enced on your way to the neighborhood water pump: Parades of horse-drawn carriages clip-clopped down busy streets as the animals dropped piles of manure in their path and yours. You might have passed at least one of the city's many slaugh-terhouses, where cattle were processed for food and their hides used to make leather goods. Without running water on the premises, waste from the slaughterhouses seeped into the streets.

But it was more than animal waste that made London smelly. Most Londoners at the time relieved themselves in privies or outhouses, then emptied the contents into large outdoor containment pits, or cesspools. Without a method to flush or wash away the collected waste, contents of the cesspools had to be removed . . . by hand.

Due to the grotesque nature of this work—and the time of day at which the unpleasant task was carried out—the essential workers who removed the waste from privies were known as "night soil men." Under cover of darkness, they lifted the large wooden planks covering the cesspools, skimmed the waste from the surface of the water, loaded it into wagons, and carried it away to the country to be used as fertilizer.

Cesspools

In the nineteenth century, the cellars of private homes were sometimes used as cesspools. In a number of documented cases, the waste was as deep as three feet.

For John Snow, there was simply too much that miasma theory failed to explain. For example, if cholera was caused by "bad air," why did it affect the digestive tract and not the body's respiratory system? This question led him to conclude that those who had contracted the disease must have somehow ingested what he called the "mortal poison." The Golden Square outbreak seemed to be concentrated in a particular area of the neighborhood, near a popular water pump on Broad Street. Snow began to suspect that the pump was the source.

At his home thirteen blocks from Golden Square, Snow prepared to gather more evidence to support his theory. He had been researching cholera outbreaks for years by the time the disease struck Golden Square in that late summer of 1854. He had honed his approach to the investigations over time, expanding his methods. He studied death records and even interviewed those in the path of the outbreaks, gathering data about their lifestyles and daily activities. John Snow the physician had moved beyond thinking about outbreaks like a doctor. Now he was thinking about outbreaks like a detective! If he could use these investigative methods to prove that the pump was the source of contamination, he might be able to convince the board of governors to intervene. And so, while the residents of Golden Square fled for their lives or isolated themselves inside their homes, John Snow strode confidently into Golden Square, grasped the Broad Street pump's handle, and filled an empty vial with water. And although he did not immediately detect anything suspicious in the sample, Snow remained convinced that his hypothesis was correct.

In search of proof, the determined doctor launched another investigation. He walked from door to door in Golden Square, interviewing residents and taking meticulous notes. How many in their household were sick? When did they first become ill? How many had died? And most important, where did they collect their water? It was grueling, detailed work, and Snow's catalog of data deepened with each new interview. After days of research, however, contradictions emerged in the evidence he gathered. A number of people who lived or worked close to the Broad Street pump had not gotten sick with cholera. Stranger still, a woman who had died of cholera lived nowhere near the pump. Snow knew that in order to build an airtight case against the Broad Street pump, he would have to account for the inconsistencies in his research.

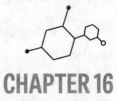

CHAPTER 16

The Cases of the Brewery, the Workhouse, and the Widow

A brewery situated east of the Broad Street pump employed seventy workers, but none of them had contracted cholera during the outbreak. From its proprietor, Mr. Huggins, Snow learned that the brewery had its own well on the premises. And brewery employees supplemented their daily water intake with samples of the malt liquor they produced.

On nearby Poland Street, the St. James Workhouse was home to 535 people, yet only five deaths were recorded there. Workhouses, intended to provide jobs and shelter for those who were unable to provide for themselves, often housed people under miserable and crowded conditions. Why hadn't more died? Snow's investigation revealed that, like the brewery, the workhouse had its own well. The five people who had died of cholera had all been recent arrivals who had contracted the illness before they were admitted to the work-house.

Finally, Snow needed to explain the mysterious death of the widow. The fifty-nine-year-old woman died of cholera on September 2, 1854, during the height of the Broad Street outbreak, but she lived in the Hampstead district, miles from Golden Square. How had she contracted cholera if she lived so far away? Snow interviewed the woman's son. He reported that his mother preferred the taste of the Broad Street pump's water and had it delivered regularly to her home in Hampstead. The widow had received a shipment of water on Thursday, August 31. Two days later, she was dead.

By Wednesday, September 6, so many residents of Golden Square had died or evacuated that the number of daily cholera cases was declining, and Snow's investigation was drawing to a close. His notes were filled with data that supported his theory that the pump was the source of the outbreak. It was time for the doctor turned disease detective to reveal his findings to the authorities. The next day, Snow presented his evidence to the board of governors. It pointed directly to the pump, but still failed to convince every member that it was the outbreak's source. Nevertheless, the board ruled that the pump's handle should be removed to prevent anyone from accessing the water below it. Cholera cases continued to decline in the days that followed and eventually the outbreak ended.

It the aftermath of the tragedy, Snow continued to refine his investigation techniques. Over the next several months, he theorized that there was a better way to communicate the information he had gathered about the outbreak. It was one thing to *tell* the board of governors about his evidence. But more and more, Snow began to imagine ways to *show* his evidence. He could see the patterns in the outbreak—that the disease had been mostly concentrated in the areas closest to the pump. If he could illustrate these patterns, it would be possible to view the entire outbreak, and its patterns, at a glance.

Eventually he plotted the cases on a common "spot map," highlighting street names and the location of every water pump in Golden Square. The locations where people died were indicated by a heavy black line. In cases where multiple people died at the same address, the black lines were stacked, one on top of the other. A person viewing the map could easily see that the greatest concentration of deaths occurred in the area of the Broad Street pump.

Snow later revised his map's design to include more details. He depicted the routes walked by Golden Square residents in and around the Broad Street pump. It was an early example of what we now call "information design." Snow was using a visual medium—a map—to portray scientific data that supported his evidence-based theory: cholera was transmitted through contaminated drinking water. But Snow's detective work and maps did more than reveal the source and impact of the outbreak. They ultimately revealed how the lives—and health—of the people of Golden Square were closely intertwined.

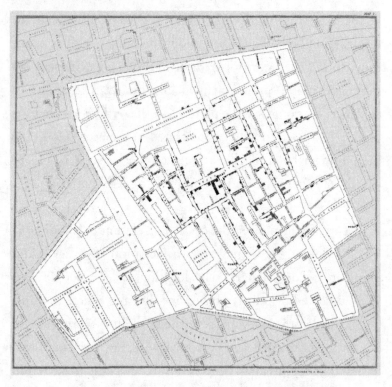

John Snow's spot map that revolutionized outbreak investigations.

Despite the ongoing resistance to his work in 1854, John Snow was not only correct about the source of the Golden Square outbreak, he was an epidemiologist ahead of his time. Today's epidemiologists still use maps to illustrate the location, scope, and severity of an outbreak within a population of people. But during his lifetime, neither Snow's data nor its depiction in maps was enough to dispel the miasma theory of disease, or to persuade everyone that the Broad Street pump was the indisputable source of the outbreak.

CHAPTER 17

Another Disease Detective

Twenty-six-year-old Reverend Henry Whitehead was among those who disagreed with John Snow about the Broad Street pump. Like other Golden Square residents, Whitehead was frustrated because he could no longer access the refreshing water from his favorite neighborhood well. The reverend decided he would conduct his own investigation to prove that Snow was wrong.

Whitehead had close ties with the people of Golden

Reverend Henry Whitehead

Square because of his position in the local church. Without any formal scientific training, he relied on his knowledge of the community to inform his investigation. Like Snow, the reverend interviewed residents and gathered as much information as he could about the outbreak. Unlike Snow, however, Whitehead knew the residents who had fled Golden Square when the epidemic started and was able to interview them as well. He spoke with hundreds of people throughout his investigation. But the more Whitehead learned, the more convinced he became that Dr. Snow was right. The two disease detectives combined their research and began working together.

While reviewing death records, Whitehead uncovered another original and crucial piece of evidence concerning the death of a five-month-old child who lived at 40 Broad Street and died during the outbreak on September 2. The document stated that the infant perished after "an attack of [diarrhea] four days previous to death." If the baby had been ill with cholera for a period of four days prior to her death on September 2, Whitehead realized she must have been sick *before* the outbreak started on August 31. Could the infant have been the very first case?

He spoke to the child's mother, Sarah Lewis, to learn more about her baby's fatal illness. Lewis told Whitehead that on the morning of August 28, the infant had been unwell, suffering from severe diarrhea. Lewis had repeatedly changed her daughter's diapers, soaking the soiled linens in a basin. Sometime later, she emptied the dirty water into the building's cesspool.

Whitehead was stunned by two pieces of information in Sarah Lewis's story. First, her daughter had fallen ill a full day earlier than what was recorded in her death record. Second, water that had been used to launder the baby's soiled diapers was emptied into the building's cesspool—a few feet from the Broad Street pump. Somehow, the soiled diaper water must have seeped from the cesspool into the well.

Whitehead's discovery prompted a further investigation. A surveyor was called to inspect the structure of the cesspool. He found that the bricks lining its walls were crumbling to pieces. The raw sewage had escaped the cesspool and leaked into the water supply. The reverend's amateur detective work had uncovered exactly how, when, and with whom the outbreak had started. In discovering that the Lewis infant was the first to die, he had stumbled upon what epidemiologists now call the index case. It had been the soiled diapers of a desperately ill child that had inadvertently contaminated the water below the Broad Street pump, causing the deaths of more than 600 people in just two weeks.

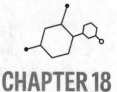

CHAPTER 18

The Legacy of John Snow and Henry Whitehead

John Snow died in 1858, before his groundbreaking research on cholera was widely accepted. But the legacy of his work with Henry Whitehead goes beyond the story of a single disease.

On the surface, the two men had little in common. Snow was a gifted doctor who believed only in what he could observe and test. Whitehead was a pastor, a man whose deep beliefs led him to trust in that which he could not see. And yet Snow's and Whitehead's investigations into the 1854 cholera outbreak would change the world. By designing plans to canvass afflicted neighborhoods, interview residents, map the outbreak, and identify the index case, Snow and Whitehead helped lay the foundation for modern epidemiology. Epidemiologists around the world continue to rely on the pioneering methods developed by Snow and Whitehead. Their story illustrates the power of one individual to make a difference during a public health crisis, and how ordinary people, initially divided by their beliefs, can find common ground and unite to protect the health and welfare of their community.

Cholera continues to pose a threat, despite John Snow's discovery and everything that we have learned about the disease since his death. The bacteriologist Robert Koch first isolated the comma-shaped bacterium that causes cholera in 1883, eventually proving that it was a type of bacteria, not "bad air," that caused it. After Koch's discovery, miasma theory was gradually replaced by germ theory.

In the 1960s, researchers in Bangladesh developed a highly effective rehydration treatment for cholera patients. The administering of this simple, lifesaving combination of water, sugar, and salt can halt the deadly dehydration caused by the disease. There are now multiple vaccines that prevent cholera. And yet, in the twenty-first century, the WHO estimates that there could be as many as 2.9 million cases and 95,000 global deaths from cholera annually in regions of Africa, India, Pakistan, the Philippines, Syria, and Haiti.

In spite of lifesaving scientific advancements, there aren't enough resources to treat every case of cholera globally. Social and environmental problems continue to create breeding grounds for bacteria. Climate change causes heavier rainfall in some areas. Catastrophic flooding and water pollution further complicate the treatment of cholera and other illnesses, while famine and multiple ongoing refugee crises can also limit access to potable water. In these areas, preventable and curable diseases like cholera continue to threaten the world's most vulnerable populations.

Filippo Pacini's Early and Hidden Discovery of Cholera

Italian scientist Filippo Pacini was studying cholera at the same time as John Snow. Through his microscope, he observed an organism that he believed to be the cause of cholera, and called it "vibrio." He published his findings but his paper went unrecognized for many years. Scholars say it's doubtful that Snow or Koch would have known about Pacini's early and unreported discovery of the organism that causes cholera.

Aid workers administer an oral cholera vaccine to Syrian children in 2023.

Among the greatest threats to life and health is one designed by human beings: war. But during the final years of World War I, the greatest threat to human life was not battlefield violence. It was a virus—a pandemic influenza that swept across the continents and killed more people than the war itself.

In the early 1950s, one young scientist set off in search of the mysterious flu's origins, hoping to learn what had made it so deadly and develop a vaccine against it. He did not know it at the time, but his search would take nearly fifty years.

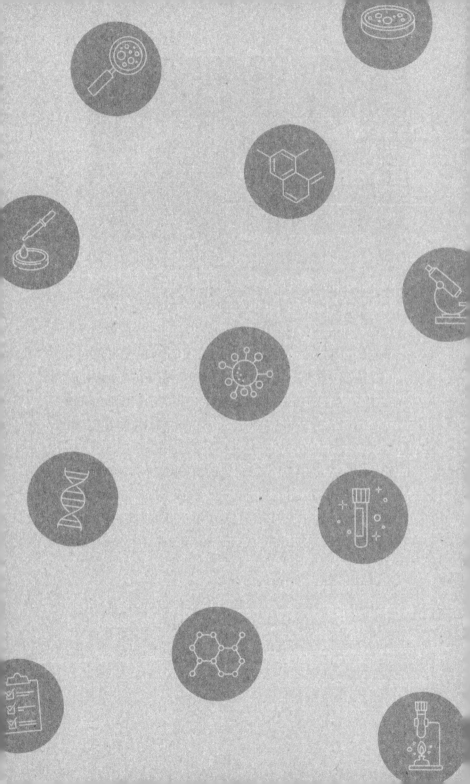

PART III

THE HUNT FOR
THE 1918 FLU

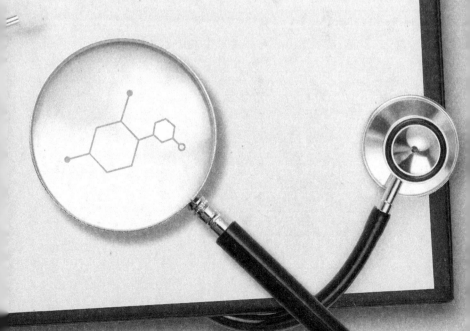

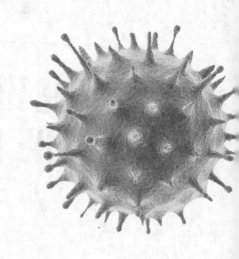
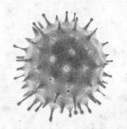

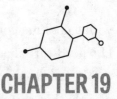

CHAPTER 19

Roscoe Vaughan and the "Knock-Me-Down Flu"

Camp Jackson, South Carolina
Thursday, September 19, 1918

US Army private Roscoe Vaughan felt awful, sicker than he ever had before. Just a few weeks earlier, the twenty-one-year-old New Yorker had reported to Camp Jackson, an army training camp crowded with 38,000 soldiers. Vaughan, like tens of thousands of young American men, was preparing to fight in World War I. From every corner of the country, recruits poured into hastily constructed training camps. President Woodrow Wilson proclaimed that America's entry into the war would "make the world safe for democracy." He couldn't have known that America's soldiers would contribute to the deaths of tens of millions of people worldwide without ever picking up a weapon.

The battlefields of Europe would have been the last thing on Private Vaughan's mind that day. He reported to sick call with a choking cough, violent chills racking his aching body. His head throbbed as the fever climbed. The soldiers called it the "knock-me-down flu." The camp doctor agreed that it was flu, but this outbreak was different. Flu viruses usually attacked the very young and the elderly, who were most vulnerable. This influenza, however, struck people between the ages of twenty and forty with astonishing speed and severity. The day that Private Vaughan reported his illness, eighty-two other soldiers had already been admitted to the camp hospital with flu symptoms. The doctor added Vaughan to his growing list of patients, jotting a quick two-word note in his medical record: "Opinion: influenza."

First Wave
Spring 1918

Earlier that spring, the mysterious flu found fertile ground to spread at Camp Funston in Fort Riley, Kansas, home to 56,000 troops. Within a month, over 1,000 soldiers were ill. Within the close quarters of the barracks, the virus spread unchecked because there were no treatments for it. At the time of the outbreak, no one knew the flu was caused by a virus. Effective vaccines and antiviral medications were not yet available because doctors mistakenly believed that a bacterium called Pfeiffer's bacillus was the culprit. The influenza virus would not be isolated and identified by British researchers until 1933, and Alexander Fleming would not discover the first antibiotic, penicillin, until 1927, so antibiotics to

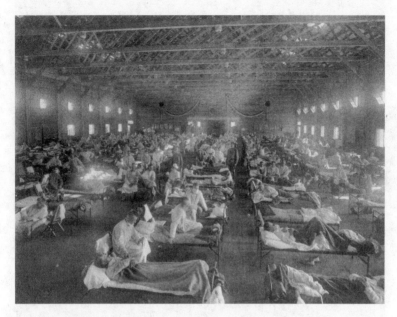

American soldiers sick with the flu in the Camp Funston, Kansas, hospital during the 1918 pandemic.

treat the severe bacterial pneumonia that could accompany influenza were still years away.

As America's troops headed for port cities to set sail for the battlefields of Europe, the virus continued to spread. By late spring, the flu had been reported in twenty-four of the army's thirty-six main camps. It had also spread to the civilian population.

In April, as US troops arrived in France to fight "the war to end all wars," the virus arrived with them. Along the war's 500-mile Western Front, which spanned France and Belgium, the flu virus flourished along with other ailments—dysentery, fevers, and lice. Within four months, the flu swept the globe in what would later be known as the "first wave" of the 1918 influenza pandemic.

The So-Called Spanish Flu

News of the deadly influenza was first reported by Spanish newspapers when the virus struck the country in May and June of 1918. The newspaper articles led to false assumptions that the outbreak had started in Spain, and that the country was disproportinately affected by the virus. In fact, it had been spreading around the world for months.

The warring countries that comprised the Allies and Central Powers censored their newspapers because they did not want the enemy to know that the flu was decimating their troops. It was considered a military secret. But Spain was a neutral country during World War I, and its newspapers were free to report on the outbreak. As a result, the virus became known as "Spanish flu," an inaccurate, derogatory, and stigmatizing term.

Second Wave
Fall 1918

By August, there were reports of a deadlier form of the influenza circulating in France, Sierra Leone, and the US. A second wave of the pandemic began to swell. Today, we know that the close quarters shared by soldiers fighting in the trenches of World War I helped the virus to mutate and spread. The fatal new flu swept back and forth between continents as troops were shipped to and from the battlefield.

Back on the home front, Private Vaughan was fighting for his life against the flu. With each passing day, breathing grew more difficult. His skin appeared blue from the lack of oxygen. Seven days after he was first admitted to the camp hospital, Private Vaughan died. It was unusual for healthy men to die from the flu, so camp doctors conducted autopsies on some of the bodies, including Vaughan's. Tissue was taken from both his lungs, preserved with formaldehyde, and placed in blocks of paraffin about the size of a small fingernail. The samples were then shipped to the Army Medical Museum for storage.

The pandemic peaked in the fall of 1918. Globally, people died by the tens of millions. According to historian Christian W. McMillen, "Within a few months, the second wave had washed over nearly every inhabited place on the planet." Scientists and historians estimate the global death toll at 50 million people, a staggering number achieved in less than twelve months. The deadliest period of the pandemic was between October and November 1918. In the United States, 675,000 people died. Of those, approximately 200,000 perished in October alone.

Overseas, the death toll skyrocketed. In India, 18 million people perished. In New Zealand, Australia, and the United States, the mortality rate of Indigenous people "was as much as four times greater than the surrounding populations," due

A 1918 San Francisco court proceeding was held outside to minimize potential spread of the flu virus.

to factors such as preexisting health conditions, insufficient housing, overwhelmed caregivers, and limited access to quality medical treatment. In China and across the continent of Africa, lack of records makes it impossible to accurately estimate the number of pandemic deaths. In fact, some historians caution that the global death estimate of 50 million could actually be closer to 100 million.

The pandemic's third wave began later that winter, eventually subsiding in the summer of 1919. By the following year, most of the world's population had been infected or died in the worst flu pandemic in human history. But where did the deadly 1918 pandemic virus come from? What kind

Racism and discrimination prevented courageous Black nurses from serving in the Army Nurse Corps during World War I. After the intensification of the 1918 flu, they were finally allowed to treat patients. Nine of the first eighteen African American women to serve in the ANS are pictured here: Clara A. Rollins, Sophia A. Hill, Marion H. Brown, Lillian F. Ball, S. Milward Boulding, N. Jeannette Minnis, Lillian Spears, Aileen B. Cole, and C. Jeannet West.

of flu virus was it? Why did it kill so many people? Could the virus hold clues to preventing a future flu pandemic? For decades, it remained a mystery. Until 1950, when a daring young medical student turned virus hunter began the search for clues.

Anti-Masking League, San Francisco

In Autumn 1918, a number of American cities (San Francisco, Oakland, Sacramento, Pasadena, Seattle, and Denver) mandated that their citizens wear masks in an effort to slow or stop the spread of the disease. Not everyone agreed with the mask ordinances, however. In San Francisco, a refusal to comply with the mask order could be punished with a $5 fine or a ten-day jail sentence. By December, an Anti-Mask League had formed. Its members questioned the necessity and effectiveness of masking. The masks worn in 1918 would not have been 100 percent effective at preventing infection because the virus particles are infinitesimally small. But as historian Alfred Crosby writes, the masks could have caught "some of the motes of dust and [droplets] of water on which the virus may [have been] riding."

When mask ordinances went into effect in public and private businesses during the COVID-19 pandemic, anti-masking rhetoric reemerged. Many people opposed the mask rules, even though

scientific data would prove that wearing a mask was an effective method of slowing the spread of the coronavirus.

A city of San Francisco police officer confronts an unmasked person.

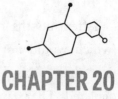

CHAPTER 20

The Fossil Hunters

Summer 1949

Digging up the massive sixteen-foot-long tusks of a woolly mammoth was not how Johan Hultin and his wife, Gunvor, had imagined spending their first summer in America. The young couple were budding scientists, not fossil hunters. They had arrived in the US in the spring of 1949 from their native Sweden to continue their studies at the University of Iowa. Johan would pursue a PhD in microbiology in addition to his medical degree. Gunvor would study radiation biology. Until the fall term began, they planned to explore the country's storied landscapes. Money was tight for the Hultins when they first arrived. In Arizona, they borrowed a car from Gunvor's relatives and embarked on an epic cross-country road trip, eventually setting foot in all forty-eight states. To save money, they camped beneath the stars.

After months of travel, the Hultins arrived in Alaska (which would not earn US statehood until 1959). By the time they reached Fairbanks, their travel fund was almost depleted. That's where they first met a gregarious German naturalist named Otto Geist, who made the Hultins an offer they couldn't refuse: in exchange for helping him with paleontological fieldwork, he would arrange a free dormitory room for them at the University of Alaska Fairbanks. The intrepid Hultins accepted. For the last three weeks of that summer, they joined Geist on his fossil-finding expedition, navigating Alaska's Seward Peninsula by boat, plane, and on foot. The Hultins noted that Geist was a familiar and welcome presence among some Alaska Natives, with acquaintances in every village along their route. In the 1920s, Geist had lived in the home of an Iñupiaq hunter and worked as a member of his whaling crew. He studied Alaska's people, traditions, and history, as well as its terrain and paleontological past.

When their summer of fossil hunting with Geist ended, Johan and Gunvor said goodbye and set off for Iowa, where the fall term was about to begin. They couldn't have known it at the time, but Johan and Geist would soon reunite for another quest.

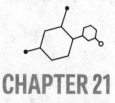

CHAPTER 21

A Germ of an Idea

The Hultins settled into their new academic life at the University of Iowa, where Johan enjoyed spending time in the laboratory with his fellow classmates. He was fascinated by the immune system and wanted to study how it responded to an influenza infection. One day, a renowned virologist, William Hale, visited the university's lab. Impressed by Hultin's work, Hale invited him to lunch with a few other students and faculty members. During the meal, the conversation turned to the 1918 pandemic, and Hale floated an idea. What if someone traveled to a cold northern climate and exhumed the bodies of people who had perished in the pandemic? It was certainly plausible, he argued, that any human remains buried beneath the arctic tundra could be well-preserved because there was a layer of permafrost—dense, rocklike frozen soil that never thawed. Those remains could, theoretically, contain organ tissue. In that case, it was also possible that a sample of the 1918 influenza virus could be found in the tissue and used for further study.

Johan Hultin's life could be measured in what came before and after Hale spoke those words. Hultin believed he was the person who should mount an expedition to find a sample of 1918 influenza. Fragments of an emerging plan ricocheted through his mind. He recalled visiting the remote areas of Alaska—places where, even in the summertime, the permafrost never fully thawed. Hultin could hardly contain his excitement.

He immediately outlined a plan and consulted his academic advisor, the virologist and associate professor Albert McKee. Hultin told McKee he wanted to travel to Alaska and search for human tissue that contained the 1918 flu virus and bring it back to the lab for further study. The project could be the basis of his PhD in microbiology. McKee agreed that the idea had potential, and Hultin quickly wrote to Otto Geist. The German replied with a list of contacts he believed would be willing to help Hultin locate grave sites of people who died in the 1918 pandemic. Hultin wrote to all of them. While he waited for replies, he continued to plan.

Using army records to survey Alaska's geography, Hultin pinpointed places where the permafrost was thick enough to preserve bodies and organ tissue. As Geist's contacts wrote to him with suggestions of where to search, Hultin narrowed his list of sites, eventually deciding on Brevig

Mission, Alaska. After a year of meticulous preparation, he departed Iowa with Albert McKee and pathologist Jack Layton. Rounding out the group was Otto Geist, who agreed to meet the Iowa team in Alaska.

The University of Iowa team bound for Alaska in 1951. From left: Johan Hultin, Jack Layton, and Albert McKee.

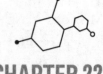

CHAPTER 22

The Alaskan Expedition

June 1951

Alaska's Seward Peninsula juts 200 miles out into the Bering Sea. It's a place where reindeer graze and Russia's coastline looms in the distance. In the winter, average temperatures can plunge to minus-ten degrees Fahrenheit—cold enough to maintain a deep layer of permafrost year-round.

The 1918 flu had arrived in some remote Alaskan villages by post, as letter carriers who traversed the region in dogsleds distributed the mail and, unknowingly, the lethal virus. Before the outbreak, the Iñupiat settlement of Brevig Mission had a population of just eighty people. When it was over, only eight of them had survived. Those seventy-two people who perished in November 1918 were buried in a mass grave. It was here, in June of 1951, that Johan Hultin would search for the virus.

The Brevig Mission, Alaska, mass grave where seventy-two people were buried after they perished in the 1918 pandemic.

The bush pilot Hultin hired kept circling, trying to find a suitable spot to land. Hultin was hoping for the beach near Brevig Mission, because he was traveling alone. The rest of his team was waiting in Fairbanks and would meet Hultin there after he had verified the quality of the permafrost and arranged to excavate the grave. But the pilot refused to risk the more convenient site, as that part of the coastline was covered with gravel. He finally landed in nearby Teller, miles from Brevig Mission, and Hultin would now have to figure out how to traverse an inlet to reach his destination.

Hultin gathered his gear, exited the plane, and was fortunate to hitch a ride across the inlet aboard a walrus-skin whaling boat. When the boat reached the shore, Hultin set out on foot. This last leg of his journey was an exhausting six-mile hike through spongy tundra, softened by the sun's warmth.

The mass grave sat on a bluff that overlooked the beach. Two large crosses marked the grave site where the seventy-two people who had lost their lives to the flu were buried. Hultin was moved by the sight of the memorial. If he could find a sample of the virus that led to the creation of a vaccine, their deaths would not have been in vain. The deep permafrost insulating the graves gave him hope.

Before he could begin the exhumation, Hultin needed permission from a woman named Jenny Olanna, a village matriarch whose opinion was revered by her community. If he could earn her trust and she agreed to the project, the town council would follow her lead and approve Hultin's request. "Fortunately for me," he recalled years later, "there were three survivors of the 1918 pandemic [who were] still alive." The survivors shared stories of how the sickness had come and killed almost everyone.

"If you allow me to enter the grave and if I'm fortunate enough to find the right specimen," Hultin told Olanna and the council, "I will take it back to my laboratory. If everything works out well, it [will] be possible for us to develop a vaccine." The possibility that a future flu pandemic could be avoided because of what might be found in the grave convinced the town council and Jenny Olanna. They granted Hultin permission for the exhumation.

Hultin began by gathering driftwood from the beach and building fires at the grave site to melt the permafrost. The sun shone for eighteen hours a day in Alaska at that time of year, and Hultin took full advantage of the light, digging in grueling sixteen-hour shifts. After two days, he had uncovered four feet of the grave and discovered the first body. It was a young girl. Her remains were in remarkably good condition, the light gray dress she was wearing the day she died still intact. It was an encouraging sign. Hultin hypothesized that remains buried deeper within the permafrost would be equally well—if not better—preserved because the ground was colder. It was time to call the rest of his team.

Geist, McKee, and Hale arrived the following day. Together, the four men dug deeper into the grave. Swarms of greedy mosquitoes feasted on the scientists as they continued their backbreaking work. Three days later, they had dug close to seven feet and discovered three more perfectly preserved bodies.

At this point, you may be wondering what, if any, measures Johan Hultin and the other scientists took to protect themselves against possible infection. They were, after all, about to remove tissue from the bodies of people who had died of a highly contagious and deadly virus. According to science writer Gina Kolata, "there were no national or international commissions ruling on the safety of what these men were doing. There were no ethics committees or lawyers deciding how to ethically or legally protect the [Indigenous community] of [Brevig Mission] or the rest of the world from what might have been a catastrophe." The scientists decided for themselves how best to proceed, guided by their scientific training and experience. When the time came to retrieve the samples, Hultin and the others used basic, proven methods of infection control to safeguard themselves and others. They cleared the area of bystanders, so they were alone when the bodies were exposed. They wore personal protective equipment (PPE), including surgical masks and gloves, while handling the bodies and samples. But recalling the events of that day years later unsettled Hultin: "We should have been more concerned about not starting this pandemic again." After retrieving the tissue as safely as they could at the time, the team closed the grave once more. Hultin snapped a few photographs of the site and thanked the villagers. Then he and his colleagues boarded a plane for home.

When Hultin's team began their expedition, they carried dry ice to preserve their samples. By the time they were ready to leave, it had evaporated. Hultin engineered a clever solution. "I remembered that when you use carbon dioxide fire extinguishers, that white cloud that comes out is dry ice, in powder form," he said. He purchased several of the devices for the return trip to Iowa. During the long plane ride, the small DC-3 made multiple stops to refuel. Each time the plane landed, the scientists grabbed the fire extinguishers and sample containers, walked some distance from the plane, and blasted them with the dry ice to keep the specimens cold.

CHAPTER 23

The Iowa Experiments

At home in the university laboratory, dressed in a protective face mask and gown, Hultin began his research by dicing the lung tissue he'd retrieved from Alaska. He added it to a saline solution and placed it inside a centrifuge. The device spun the sample solution at a high rate of speed, the force of gravity separating the virus particles out of the solution. Next, he injected the virus material into hundreds of fertilized chicken eggs. It was a tedious process. A one-half square inch of the eggshell had to be carefully cut away without ruptur-ing the thin membrane beneath it. Hultin injected the virus material into the white of the egg. If the amniotic fluid inside the eggs turned cloudy, he would know he had succeeded in growing the virus. All this work took place under a nega-tive pressure hood. If there was any live influenza virus in the specimens, the hood would prevent it from being released into the room.

Scientists began growing influenza inside chicken eggs in the 1930s. Seven decades later, the practice continues as part of the large-scale manufacturing of vaccines. A virus is injected into an egg, where it grows or replicates. It is then extracted from inside the egg, purified, and killed. The killed virus becomes the antigen—the substance in the vaccine that kick-starts the production of antibodies by the immune system. If a vaccinated person encounters that particular flu virus, the body knows how to defend against it.

However, after injecting a multitude of eggs, Hultin and lab technician Sally Whitney hadn't managed to grow the virus inside any of them. He next attempted to infect mice and ferrets, but those experiments failed as well. "Week after week after week I got more discouraged," he said, and within six weeks, he had no specimens left. Hultin was devastated. His dream of reviving the 1918 flu to create a vaccine was dead—and so were his hopes of using the research to earn a PhD in microbiology. "There went my PhD," he said. "I could see it fly right out of the window."

Hultin packed up his research and resolved to let other scientists search for the elusive virus. And because his experiments had failed, he did not publish any articles about his early work on the 1918 flu in scientific journals. Hultin went on to graduate from medical school at the University of Iowa, then settled in the United States, building a successful career as a pathologist until he retired in 1988. As the years passed, he continued to read scientific journals about virology. One day, he believed, another virus hunter would embark on the same search for the 1918 flu and succeed where he had failed.

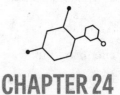

CHAPTER 24

Dr. Taubenberger's Time Machine

Armed Forces Institute of Pathology
Bethesda, Maryland
1997

Inside the Armed Forces Institute of Pathology (AFIP), the journal club gathered for its weekly meeting. The scientists met to discuss interesting articles they'd read in scientific journals. Among the attendees was thirty-six-year-old pathologist Dr. Jeffery Taubenberger, a quiet, patient scientist who also enjoyed composing classical music.

While his high school classmates had prepared for their senior year, Jeffery, the future scientist, began college a year early. He eventually studied medicine, became a doctor, and earned a PhD in biology. He loved working at an esteemed government facility where he was surrounded by colleagues who shared his devotion to science. He hoped they would also share his enthusiasm for the article he was about to present at the journal club meeting.

The subject was the groundbreaking nineteenth-century chemist John Dalton. Everyone in the room knew Dalton's name—he had formulated the modern atomic theory of matter that is the foundation for the study of modern chemistry. Dalton was also color-blind. The distinguished scientist left instructions that after he died, his eyes should be removed and preserved for research. His wishes were followed to the letter. Sealed inside a glass jar, Dalton's eyeballs became the property of the John Dalton Society of Great Britain.

In 1995, a group of researchers obtained a sample of Dalton's eye tissue from the society. Using recently developed PCR testing to amplify a segment of DNA in the eye tissue, they were able to confirm the type of color-blindness that afflicted Dalton. It was "clever and cute," Taubenberger said, "but didn't really advance medicine." And that's what he wanted to do, Taubenberger told his colleagues—advance medicine with a project that would highlight the AFIP's tissue archive. The collection was a treasure trove of 3 million specimens. It had been established during the Civil War by President Abraham Lincoln as the Army Medical Museum to study wartime illness and disease.

Taubenberger began brainstorming ideas for a project with his colleagues. The eureka moment came when someone suggested he study the 1918 pandemic influenza virus. It was the perfect subject to showcase the AFIP archive because important questions still remained unanswered about the deadly flu. No one knew what type of flu virus it was or why it had been so deadly for young people between the ages of twenty and forty. Taubenberger would use his training as a pathologist to analyze samples taken from soldiers who had died in the pandemic. Utilizing the tools of modern pathology and molecular biology, he would attempt to reconstruct the virus's genetic sequence. While the John Dalton eye study that inspired him had been an interesting scientific exercise, Taubenberger hoped his exploration of the 1918 flu could uncover important data about the virus that might inform responses to future influenza outbreaks.

Taubenberger didn't know much about the 1918 pandemic and soon learned that he was not alone. Despite the fact that it had killed at least 50 million people worldwide, the 1918 influenza was a forgotten pandemic. He turned to history books to discover why the pandemic had slipped into obscurity. According to historian Alfred Crosby, the ferocious virus had extinguished itself relatively quickly, in about a year. The pandemic had also occurred during a time of tremendous global upheaval as World War I dominated the headlines. Among popular history textbooks, Crosby wrote in 1989, only one mentioned the pandemic at all—a single sentence that "understat[ed] the total number of deaths due to it by at least one-half."

Dr. Taubenberger was inspired. "A pandemic of this magnitude, that impacted everything on earth, certainly affected all fields of human endeavor," he said. "For me, as a physician, the important thing is what we can learn about what happened in the past to try and apply that knowledge . . . to prevent something like this from ever happening again."

Two months later, Taubenberger and his colleague Ann Reid began the tedious task of trying to reconstruct the 1918 influenza's unique gene sequence, or genome.

Drs. Taubenberger and Reid examine their data in the search for genetic traces of the 1918 pandemic flu virus.

CHAPTER 25

"Chance of Success . . . Extremely Remote"

Imagine that an alien from another planet decides to build a human being from scratch. It is going to need a book of instructions. Your genome is that book. Composed of DNA, it's like a cellular operating manual for the human body. Contained within it is every piece of genetic information that makes you, *you*—from the color of your hair and eyes to your ability to grow and mature over time. According to yourgenome.org, a printout of the human genome "would fill a stack of paperback books 200 feet high . . . and take a century to recite at one letter per second for 24 hours a day." Every organism has its own unique genome, including viruses. Unlike you, however, a virus is not alive. It's a simple bundle of genetic material, composed of either DNA or RNA, surrounded by a shell of protein that protects its machinery while the virus attempts to infect cells.

Taubenberger and Reid were hopeful that they would succeed in sequencing the virus's genome, but they knew the chances were slim. Managing expectations was crucial because what they were attempting to accomplish was going to take time. "Science moves at a much slower pace," Taubenberger once said. "You have a much longer-term sense of gratification." The scientists began their work by requesting lung tissue samples from the AFIP archive of seventy soldiers who died of influenza in 1918, the deadliest year of the pandemic.

The eighty-seven-year-old samples arrived in brown paper bags, each labeled with a case number, along with the autopsy reports. For months the scientists probed the samples for any sign of the virus but found nothing. After almost a year of work, Dr. Taubenberger decided to narrow their search criteria. Without antibiotics to treat pneumonia in 1918, the bacterial infection would have set in as a life-threatening secondary condition. The onset of pneumonia would have hastened death, so Taubenberger decided to include only those cases in which the soldier exhibited signs of bacterial pneumonia and died within a week of getting sick. The shorter the term of illness, the more likely it was that they would find traces of the virus in the tissue. A total of seven tissue samples fit the new search criteria. Only one contained traces of the virus. It belonged to twenty-one-year-old US Army private Roscoe Vaughan.

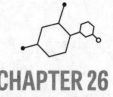

CHAPTER 26

The Legacy of Roscoe Vaughan

Private Vaughan's tissue sample gave Taubenberger and Reid hope because the soldier's left lung was consumed by the bacterial pneumonia that had killed him. Tissue taken from his right lung was not. This was an encouraging sign because the virus in the right lung had been in the early stages at the soldier's time of death. That meant there was a small chance that they would be able to detect RNA (the genetic material of influenza viruses) in that lung.

The amount of preserved material in the paraffin block was impossibly small. The scientists carefully shaved thin slices from the block that were barely the width of a red blood cell. Through meticulous work, they filtered the tissue and found what they had been searching for: fragmented pieces of the virus's RNA.

Influenza viruses are composed of eight genes. Tauben-berger and Reid had found RNA fragments of five of them. Reid used a PCR machine to make millions of molecular copies of the incomplete pieces of RNA. Next, those copies were used to compare the 1918 virus's genes to the genetic sequences of all other known influenzas. They did not find a match. Taubenberger and Reid had discovered that the 1918 influenza virus was unique. It was a H1N1 type virus: *H* for hemagglutinin and *N* for neuraminidase. These two genes are crucial to the survival of all influenza virus types because they help the virus get into and out of cells. In order to survive, the first thing any virus must do is gain access to a healthy cell. With influenza, that is the job of the *H* gene. Like a key, it unlocks the cell. Once inside, the virus hijacks its machinery, forcing the cell to make more copies of the virus. After the cell is filled with new virus particles, they must escape. This exit strategy is controlled by the *N* gene. Its job is to rupture the hijacked cell to release the new copies, spreading the virus.

Research suggests that the 1918 H1N1 flu virus had entered the human population from pigs but may have originally descended from birds. Bird flus, or avian influenza viruses, usually originate in wild migratory water birds and some poultry species. Like hantaviruses, they are zoonotic, able to spread between people and animals. Before reaching humans, these avian influenza viruses sometimes hop into an intermediate animal host, like pigs. As the virus jumps from animal to animal and species to species, it can change or mutate. Sometimes those mutations make it possible for viruses to jump into people. If a virus can further mutate inside the bodies of human beings over time, it may become transmissible from person to person. When this happens, it can cause a pandemic.

In the past 100 years there have been three other outbreaks of pandemic influenza: 1957, 1968, and 2009. All of them paled in comparison to the devastation caused by the 1918 flu. Eerily, according to Dr. Taubenberger, it is still with us. "Since 1918," he said, "all pandemic influenza and seasonal viruses descended from the 1918 virus." His assertion offers a chilling perspective on the number of people who have died because of the historic outbreak. "It's not just that tens of millions of people died in about a year's time . . . there are millions and millions of people who have died of flu in the last 100-plus years, all as a result of a single importation of [what was] likely a zoonotic event into humans."

In March 1997, Taubenberger and Reid published their results in the prestigious journal *Science*, but more work was required if they were going to succeed in their longer-term goal of sequencing the virus's complete genome. In the meantime, they had exhausted their entire supply of 1918 lung tissue, so their ambitious project was suspended indefinitely.

CHAPTER 27

More Than a Medical Detective Story

While Taubenberger and Reid considered where they would find more specimens of the 1918 influenza, Johan Hultin was enjoying retirement in San Francisco, California. He continued to read medical journals and other publications about the field of virology, always hoping that another scientist would undertake the search for the 1918 influenza. He was scanning a copy of *Science News* for updates from the world of medical research when a headline on page 172 leaped from the page: "A [Soldier's] Lungs Yield 1918 Flu Virus."

The brief article summarized the 1918 influenza study that Dr. Jeffery Taubenberger and Dr. Ann Reid had recently published. "This is not just a medical detective story," Dr. Taubenberger told the interviewer. "This could happen again. It would be really useful to find out what happened in 1918 and apply that knowledge to protect us against future outbreaks." Hultin could not have agreed more. It had taken forty-six years, but another scientist was finally searching for the 1918 influenza!

Hultin immediately wrote to Taubenberger, describing his trip to Alaska in 1951. He told the scientist that he believed the bodies preserved in the permafrost at Brevig Mission, Alaska, might still contain traceable amounts of the 1918 flu. Not only did he know where to find more samples, he was willing to travel to Alaska to retrieve them. Before mailing the letter, Hultin added a copy of his résumé to the envelope, to reassure Dr. Taubenberger that he was sincere and quali-fied to do the work. Hultin hoped Dr. Taubenberger would give him a second chance to succeed where he had failed all those years ago.

As weeks passed with no reply, Hultin's dreams of a sec-ond hunt for the virus in Alaska began to fade. He imagined the young scientist receiving the letter and dismissing it as the ramblings of a foolish old man who was sticking his nose where it didn't belong. In late summer, he finally received a letter from Taubenberger, who had been away from the office because his wife had given birth to their child. He assured Hultin that he was equally excited by the possibilities, and eager to accept the generous offer to retrieve more specimens. The retired virus hunter was overjoyed. Finally, he was back on the hunt for the 1918 flu.

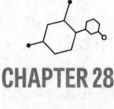

CHAPTER 28
Back to Brevig

August 1997

With $3,200 of his own money in his pocket to finance the dig, Johan Hultin arrived in Alaska for the second time. He knew from experience that he would have to obtain permission to enter the grave, but there were no guarantees. A local pastor, Brian Crockett, volunteered to help Hultin. There were no hotels in town, so the pastor arranged for him to sleep on an air mattress in the community's school. Next, he introduced Hultin to the people in Brevig who would have to approve his request to exhume bodies at the mass grave. One of them was Rita Olanna, the granddaughter of Jenny Olanna, the matriarch whose approval Hultin had won on his previous trip. Like her grandmother, Rita Olanna agreed that he should be allowed to reenter the grave. With her blessing, Hultin addressed the town council. He talked about his first trip to Brevig Mission in 1951, describing how science had advanced since then. He told them that his work at the grave site might one day lead to a vaccine that would prevent a similar pandemic.

Like Rita and Jenny Olanna, the town council agreed that Hultin should be allowed to exhume the bodies and offered their help. Four young men from the village were assigned to assist him at the grave site. Although Hultin had been athletic his entire life (at the age of fifty-eight, he ascended a 25,000-foot mountain on skis), he was now seventy-two years old and gratefully accepted the assistance. It felt appropriate that the four young men, all Iñupiat, help preside over the excavation of the grave.

It was August in Alaska. Hultin knew that the ground would be much more forgiving in late summer than it had been on his previous visit. Using the old photograph he had taken after closing the grave all those years ago, Hultin marked off the area where he would dig. On the second day, at a depth of about seven feet, he found what he was searching for: the body of an Iñupiaq woman, perfectly preserved in the permafrost.

After his first failed attempt at isolating the 1918 influenza, Hultin had repeatedly said that he was "the right man, in the right place, at the wrong time." Now, as he looked into her grave, he realized he might finally be in the right place at the right time. Layers of fat still present inside her body helped preserve her tissue against the ravages of time and the freezing/thawing cycles of the tundra. Inside her chest cavity, the lungs were beautifully preserved. Seated on an over-turned bucket, Hultin carefully removed the tissue, storing the samples in preservatives provided by Dr. Taubenberger.

When Hultin's work was complete, he and the four volunteers restored the grave. He paid the men and thanked them for their help. One task remained, and Hultin wanted to finish it on his own. The two original crosses that once marked the mass grave had disappeared since his last visit to Brevig. Using his photograph from 1951 as a guide once again, he purchased some lumber and spent the rest of the evening constructing new ones. The next morning, with the help of local high school students, the crosses were erected at the grave site. Hultin hoped his gift expressed the depth of his gratitude to the people of Brevig. For the second time in his life, Johan Hultin left Alaska filled with hope that his discovery would yield new information about the 1918 flu.

Before shipping the samples to Dr. Taubenberger, Hultin had carefully divided the lung tissue into four separate packages as a safety precaution. The material was far too valuable to send in a single shipment. After each of the boxes had been safely received by Taubenberger, Hultin waited to hear if the scientists found evidence of influenza in the lung specimens.

Hultin was surprised when he received a telephone call soon after his return to San Francisco. The second trip to Brevig had been a huge success, Taubenberger said. He and Reid had found genetic evidence of the 1918 influenza in the woman's lung tissue, and thanks to Hultin they now had more than enough tissue to work with. Hultin was elated. But he and the other scientists knew this was only the next small step down a long road. The first had been finding the virus in the preserved lung tissue of Private Roscoe Vaughan. The work that lay ahead of them—sequencing the virus's entire genome—would be a difficult and painstaking process.

It had taken nine years of work, but in 2005, Taubenberger and Reid completed the virus's genome sequence. Like a blueprint, it revealed the genetic mutations that enabled the virus to explode into a devastating pandemic. If a new influenza virus emerged in the future with similar mutations, scientists would know that it had the same pandemic potential as the 1918 flu.

The combined efforts of Taubenberger, Reid, and Hultin had resulted in a monumental achievement. But it also laid the groundwork for a more daring—and controversial—scientific study. Now that the virus's genome had been sequenced, it was also possible to resurrect the deadliest flu in human history.

Johan Hultin and Rita Olanna, reunited in 2005, view a photograph of her grandmother Jenny Olanna.

CHAPTER 29

Resurrection

Why resurrect a long-dead virus that had killed millions of people a hundred years ago? This was the question that scientists had to answer before the US government would consider allowing them to revive the deadly influenza. Whether or not the scientists' arguments were compelling enough to justify their actions is something you must judge for yourself.

Dr. Taubenberger and other advocates of resurrecting the 1918 influenza virus argued that any technology can be used to create a positive or negative outcome. Potential negative outcomes ranged from a lab accident that could infect a single scientist working with the virus, to the unthinkable: the virus somehow escaping the laboratory. Equally terrifying was the possibility that samples of the resurrected virus could accidentally fall into the hands of someone who would use it as a biological weapon.

Taubenberger acknowledged these scary possibilities but insisted that the potential rewards outweighed the calculated risks. Every precaution, he said, would be taken to ensure that the virus was not mishandled.

Those safety precautions began with the scientist selected to revive the virus in the laboratory. Only one researcher would be permitted to carry out the experiments, and that person would have to register in something called the Federal Select Agent Program. This government entity oversees the possession, use, and transfer of biological agents, like lethal viruses, that pose a public health threat. The scientist would also have to submit to a background check by the FBI and undergo regular physical and psychological evaluations. They would have to be vaccinated against influenza and take antiviral medications, like Tamiflu, to protect them in the event of accidental infection.

All these criteria would have to be met before the researcher set foot in a high-security laboratory to conduct the experiments. Laboratories are divided into four biological safety levels that correspond to how much danger the microbe being examined poses to human life. Level one microbes (such as chicken pox) are not known to consistently cause disease in adult humans. Level two microbes (like *Streptococcus pneumonia* and salmonella) pose a moderate threat to human life if exposed to the skin, inhaled, or swallowed. Level three microbes (tuberculosis, avian flu, plague) can cause serious illness and death if inhaled. Level four microbes (Lassa fever,

Ebola virus, Marburg virus, and others) are life-threatening pathogens, some of which can be transmitted through the air. Vaccines or treatments for these diseases may not be readily available.

The laboratory in which a scientist would carry out the experiments on the 1918 influenza virus was a biosafety level three (BSL-3) fortress. Its windows, doors, and walls were sealed. An elaborate airflow system ensured that clean air was constantly drawn toward contaminated areas and that no exhausted air from the lab escaped into other parts of the building.

Access to these secure containment labs is highly restricted. Those with permission must first pass through a minimum of two sets of interlocking doors. Before entering the facility, the scientist must put on personal protective equipment: a bodysuit, gloves, and a powered air-purifying respirator over their face. Some BSL-3 laboratories may also require a retinal scan to properly identify the scientist before they are allowed to enter. Once inside, the scientist would take their place at a lab table housed inside a biosafety cabinet that was equipped with a special HEPA air filter, further reducing the risk of contamination.

The discussion about whether to permit the revivification of the 1918 flu began at the Centers for Disease Control and Prevention and reached the highest levels of American government. Ultimately, both the secretary of defense as well as the secretary of health and human services were convinced that the project was worthwhile and were satisfied that it could be carried out safely. The experiments would take place at the CDC in Atlanta after regular business hours—another safety precaution. The agency tapped one of its own, the microbiologist Dr. Terrence Tumpey, for the groundbreaking and potentially dangerous scientific project.

Dr. Terrence Tumpey at work in a biosafety level 3 laboratory.

Alone inside a CDC laboratory, Dr. Tumpey began his attempt to reconstruct the 1918 influenza virus. If he succeeded, Tumpey would be the first person since the 1918 pandemic to come that close to the live virus that had killed millions. Tumpey wanted to understand what made the virus so deadly and transmissible between people, knowledge that could inform the response to future flu pandemics and possibly prevent them. Using Dr. Taubenberger's genome "blueprint," Tumpey began assembling the virus's genetic ingredients: the eight genes that comprised the 1918 influenza virus. He injected those genes into cells and waited. Three days passed. Then Tumpey began to observe structural changes in the host cells. They were dying, which could only mean one thing: Tumpey had succeeded! The deadliest influenza virus ever known had been reborn in his lab. He carefully collected the virus material and used it to make multiple aliquots—more samples—of the virus for further study.

Through his investigation, Tumpey was able to determine that the 1918 virus replicated with astounding efficiency, a fact that helped explain how it had killed tens of millions of people around the world within a year's time. He kept digging, eventually exploring which of the virus's eight genes would cause the greatest amount of disease in mammals. To find out, he individually matched each of the virus's genes to an ordinary seasonal flu virus. He discovered that the hemagglutinin gene (the gene that helps the virus unlock cells) was the most important to the success of the 1918 virus. When he placed the hemagglutinin in a nonlethal seasonal flu virus, that virus was transformed. "All of the sudden," he said, "it was lethal."

Tumpey's work led to a vaccine against the 1918 flu. When laboratory mice were vaccinated, then exposed to the virus, none of them got sick. The vaccine was 100 percent effective in preventing illness. The work of Taubenberger, Tumpey, Hultin, and Reid represented a quantum leap in scientific knowledge about the 1918 influenza. However, troubling questions remain unanswered.

CHAPTER 30

Back to the Future

Scientists still aren't certain about where in the world the 1918 influenza originated or precisely how the virus first jumped from an animal to humans. It also remains unclear why the virus decimated the population of young people between the ages of twenty and forty from 1918 to 1919. But some have a theory. Ironically, youth could have been a contributing factor to those deaths. The 1918 flu strain may have triggered an overreaction in the immune systems of young, healthy adults, precisely because their immune systems are so robust earlier in life. It's called a cytokine storm. Immune cells use specialized proteins called cytokines to communicate when the body is fighting off an intruder. If you've ever experienced a runny nose or fever when you had a cold, you have cytokines to thank for those relatively mild symptoms. But the far more severe 1918 flu could have led to an overproduction of cytokines, which caused catastrophic inflammation of the lungs. As a result, those infected with the virus were more susceptible to life-threatening secondary infections, like pneumonia, increasing their risk of death and explaining why young adults died in the greatest numbers during the pandemic.

Amid the lingering doubt surrounding the 1918 flu, one certainty remains: influenza viruses are a natural part of life on this planet. There will be another influenza pandemic—though when it will occur, or how dangerous and widespread it will be, no one knows. In the meantime, scientists continue to monitor circulating flu viruses that have pandemic potential.

Next-generation seasonal flu vaccines that are faster to produce and easier to modify than traditional flu vaccines are under development. Several universal flu vaccines—single shots that would guard against every type of flu infection—have progressed to the clinical trial stage. But until a universal vaccine becomes available, an annual flu shot is the best way to protect yourself.

Different influenza viruses circulate at different times. Every year, scientists make an educated guess as to which flu viruses the vaccine should target. Some years the shots are more effective than others, and while vaccinated people can still get sick with seasonal flu, the vaccines can decrease the risk of severe illness that could require a hospital stay or lead to death.

Seasonal Flu by the Numbers

An influenza virus doesn't have to cause a pandemic in order to be deadly. Seasonal flu kills people every year. During the 2021-2022 flu season in the United States, the CDC estimates that there were as many as 610,000 hospitalizations and 54,000 deaths because of flu. While scientists and public health professionals are on the lookout for early warning signs of a flu pandemic and developing cutting-edge vaccines, all of us can play a role in safeguarding public health. According to CDC.gov, "during 2019-2020 ... seasonal flu vaccinations prevented an estimated 7.5 million influenza illnesses, 3.7 million influenza-associated medical visits, 105,000 influenza-associated hospitalizations, and 6,300 influenza-associated deaths."

Humankind is still waging war on influenza and many other known and emerging diseases. But there is one deadly disease—for now, the only one—that humans have succeeded in eradicating: smallpox. The triumph over smallpox was the result of a global army of disease detectives and virus hunters who were determined to achieve what seemed like an impossible goal. Together, they tracked smallpox to every corner of the earth and eliminated it once and for all.

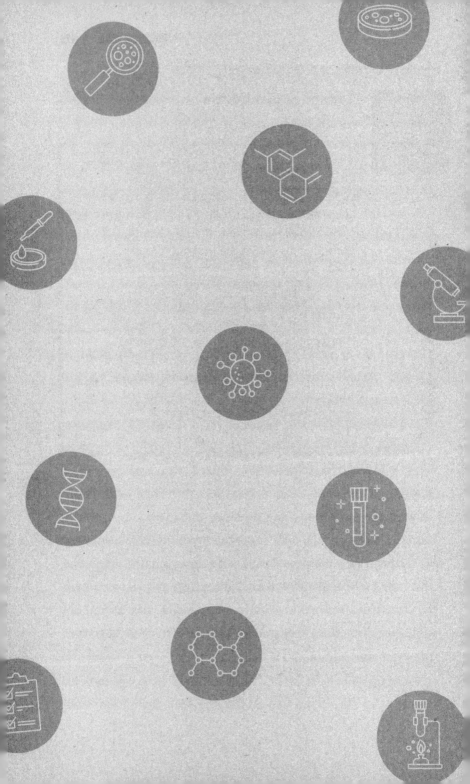

PART IV

THE SMALLPOX HUNTERS

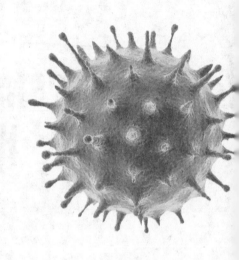

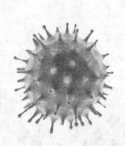

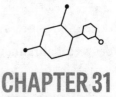

CHAPTER 31
Neil Vora and the Pox Puzzle

Tianeti, a city in the country of Georgia
2013

Dr. Neil Vora strode through a green pasture of grazing cattle. Tall, with dark hair and glasses, and dressed in a sweatshirt and jeans, Vora might have been mistaken for a tourist if he weren't wearing latex gloves and carrying swabs and plastic vials. But the scientist had not traveled to Georgia, a formerly communist country at the crossroads of Eastern Europe and Western Asia, to sight-see. He was there at the request of officials from the Georgia National Center for Disease Control and Public Health (NCDC) to assist in their country's investigation of a mysterious outbreak.

In June 2013, two otherwise healthy young men who worked with the same herd of cattle had fallen ill within ten days of each other. Both reported the appearance of itchy, painful lesions on their hands. Soon the blisters began to ooze, and more symptoms followed: a fever of at least 102 degrees Fahrenheit, chills, and body weakness. The lymph nodes of their armpits swelled into large lumps.

At first, health officials in Georgia suspected anthrax. The serious and sometimes fatal disease, caused by the bacterium *Bacillus anthracis*, is carried by wild and domestic animals, such as cattle. Anthrax can be transmitted to human beings through an open cut on the skin, by inhaling the bacterium's spores, or consuming contaminated food or drinking water. In the United States, anthrax is relatively rare. In other parts of the world—including Eastern Europe, where Georgia is located—the disease is more common.

The cattle workers tested negative for anthrax and both fully recovered, but no one knew what had made them sick. That's when the country's concerned public health officials sent samples of the virus to the Centers for Disease Control and Prevention (CDC), hoping the agency could help identify it. In Atlanta, test results revealed that the cause of the outbreak was a new type of cowpox virus. The CDC scientists also discovered that the virus was a second cousin of one of the most notorious viruses to ever attack humankind: variola, the virus that causes smallpox. Fearing this new poxvirus could be as potentially lethal as its ancestor, the CDC was invited to collaborate in a full investigation.

Dr. Neil Vora was chosen to lead the American team that deployed to Georgia. As an Epidemic Intelligence Service (EIS) officer in the Poxvirus and Rabies Branch at the CDC, poxviruses were Vora's specialty. In a matter of days, the group, along with their Georgian colleagues, had completed tests on the cattle, domesticated animals, and wildlife in the area. They uncovered evidence of previous infections in cattle and local rodents. Thankfully, no additional human cases were found, and neither was there any evidence that the new virus (later named Akhmeta virus) was lethal or transmissible from person to person.

For Neil Vora, the investigation into an outbreak of a poxvirus was more than a job. It was personal. He had become a physician and epidemiologist with the CDC because of smallpox. His father, Manhar Vora, had been born in India, a country ravaged by the disease for centuries. Manhar had contracted the disease before he was five years old. "He survived," Neil Vora said. "That's why I am here today." Vora remembers, as a child, looking up at his father's face, scarred by smallpox. It was a permanent reminder of what he had endured. Vora's father had been fortunate to escape death, because smallpox killed more children than adults.

It was Neil's father who first encouraged him to study medicine. "He told me about this organization, an agency called the Centers for Disease Control and Prevention, and it was always with the highest respect." The elder Vora told his son that he had always wanted to work for the agency, but never found the opportunity. He wanted Neil to work for the CDC someday. Neil did, too. He remembers watching the film *Outbreak* with his dad. In the fictional account, government disease detectives race against the clock to contain a killer virus spreading across the United States. The movie changed Vora's life. "I knew that was the job for me," he said. "I wanted to wear a [pressurized biosafety suit] and chase dangerous diseases around the world."

Disease detective Dr. Neil Vora and his father, Manhar

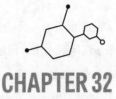

CHAPTER 32
The Fortunate Ones

You are among the most fortunate people to have ever lived on Earth. Like disease detective Neil Vora, you occupy this planet during an age when one of humankind's most dreaded diseases, smallpox, has been completely eradicated. During the twentieth century, as many as 300 million people were not as fortunate. They died of smallpox. It was a torturous death.

A person who had been infected with smallpox did not know they were sick until ten or twelve days after exposure to the variola virus. The first signs of illness were pounding headaches, body-racking chills, and blazing fevers. Muscles and limbs ached, growing heavy from extreme fatigue. Sometimes there was nausea, vomiting, and convulsions. A few days later a red rash appeared on the skin. At first it was small and flat, but as the disease progressed, the rash evolved into fluid-filled blisters. Thousands of them could spread over every inch of the body. The slightest movement was agony. Lesions of the mouth made it impossible to speak, drink, or eat. One in three people with smallpox died.

For survivors, the pustules would eventually dry up and form scabs. As the scabs fell away, they left behind deep pockmarks that permanently scarred the body and face. Many smallpox survivors were left blind from their encounter with the virus; however, by surviving smallpox, they earned lifelong immunity against the disease.

A smallpox patient, Côte d'Ivoire, 1960

CHAPTER 33

An Ancient Enemy

Smallpox is believed to have emerged around 14,000 years ago when people first began living together in agricultural communities. The exact origins of the disease are unknown because it arose before humans kept records. Among the oldest suspected cases is Egyptian king Pharaoh Ramses V, who died in 1157 BCE. His mummified body was discovered in 1898. At the time, researchers noted the presence of a rash resembling a poxvirus, hinting that smallpox infected the people of Egypt as many as 3,000 years ago.

In late 1979, CDC physician Dr. Donald R. Hopkins and Professor Mourad A. Sherif were granted permission to examine the mummy and remove a tissue sample to determine if Ramses V had smallpox. They didn't find conclusive evidence, but "after seeing [the rash] at first hand," Hopkins wrote, "I am almost as convinced that he did indeed have smallpox as if I had actually seen a three-thousand-year-old poxvirus."

The fourth-century Athenian historian Thucydides recorded his observations of the Plague of Athens, believed to have been caused by smallpox. It began in 430 BCE and lasted three years, killing as many as a quarter of the city's residents—up to 100,000 people. "The exterior of the body was . . .

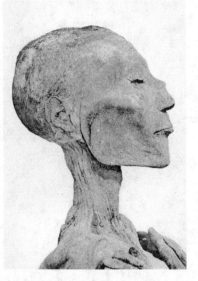

The pockmarks on the mummified body of Egyptian ruler Ramses V are believed to be smallpox scars.

reddish, livid, and burst out in small blisters and sores," Thucydides wrote. "But inside the burning was so strong that the victims could not bear to put on even the lightest clothes and linens . . ."

In the sixth century, smallpox arrived in Japan as trade expanded with China and Korea. A hundred years later, it landed in northern Africa, Spain, and Portugal. Between the fifteenth and sixteenth centuries, European colonization and the slave trade spread the disease to western Africa and the Caribbean islands, as well as Central and South America, and Australia. In the seventeenth century, European colonizers introduced the disease to North America, decimating populations of Indigenous people.

Then, in the eighteenth century, there was a break-through. For years, the English physician Dr. Edward Jenner had heard tales of folk wisdom claiming that dairy maids who had recovered from cowpox were immune to smallpox. Jenner hypothesized that he could use cowpox as a means to immunize people against its deadly cousin. At that point, there were two known ways to earn immunity against small-pox: survive it or undergo a preventative treatment known as variolation.

In this minor procedure, a small cut was made in the skin. Then a minuscule amount of infected material from a smallpox lesion was inserted into the cut and covered with a bandage. When the procedure was successful, the result was a mild case of smallpox lasting only a few days, and the patient became immune to the disease. In another procedure, scabs from a smallpox lesion could be ground into a powder, then blown into the nose through a tube. Both methods were risky. The person being variolated would be infectious—capable of spreading the disease to others. And if the variolated person accidentally received too much of the infected material during either procedure, they could die of smallpox.

In 1796, Jenner designed an experiment to test a new method. A diary maid named Sarah Nelmes gave Jenner a sample of infectious material from a cowpox lesion on her hand. He used the sample to inoculate his gardener's son, eight-year-old James Phipps, with cowpox, by placing the material into a small cut on the boy's arm. Months later, Jenner exposed Phipps to smallpox, and his hypothesis was proven correct when the boy did not contract the virus. Jenner had proven that previous exposure to cowpox had protected Phipps from the much more severe, and potentially lethal, smallpox infection.

Edward Jenner had successfully performed the world's first vaccination, and over time, his method replaced variolation. Still, as many as 400,000 people a year died of smallpox in Europe, including five reigning monarchs. In the nineteenth century, the virus threatened the life of an American president.

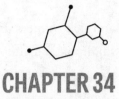

CHAPTER 34

A Pox on the Presidency

President Abraham Lincoln died on April 15, 1865, after being shot by John Wilkes Booth inside Ford's Theatre in Washington, DC. But Booth was not the first killer to attack the president.

Two years earlier on November 19, 1863, Lincoln complained of a debilitating headache. Earlier that day, he had delivered a speech that would become one of the most important in American history, the Gettysburg Address. Afterward, feeling sick, Lincoln went to bed. A rash soon broke out on his body. A doctor confirmed that the president had smallpox and placed him in quarantine.

It's unclear how Lincoln contracted smallpox. However, at the time of his illness, the United States was torn apart by the Civil War. Military hospitals were filled with wounded and sick soldiers. Historians theorize that Lincoln contracted smallpox at a Union hospital in Washington where he visited troops a couple of weeks before delivering his speech at Gettysburg.

During the ten to fourteen days before he first felt sick, while the virus was incubating in his body, Lincoln was not yet contagious. He would have been symptom-free and feeling healthy. But if the incubation period of the virus had been shorter by a single day, the president would have fallen ill sooner, and may have been too sick to deliver the Gettysburg Address. Lincoln recovered from smallpox, but there was another casualty of his illness. William Johnson was a freed Black man who worked as Lincoln's valet. In this role, he served as the president's barber and tended to his clothes. Historical accounts suggest there was a great deal of trust between the two men that expanded Johnson's duties. The president also relied on him to deliver private letters as well as money. Johnson "never hesitated" to ask the president to do things for him as well. At Johnson's request, Lincoln helped him secure a new job at the US Treasury Department.

Johnson was periodically excused from his job to attend to the president, and accompanied him to Gettysburg for Lincoln's historic speech. Historians believe Johnson would have also been the person caring for the president during his illness. Smallpox can spread through contact with the sores caused by the virus and the fluid they contain, or by contact with contaminated bedding or clothing. The virus can also be transmitted through droplets that are released when a person with smallpox coughs or sneezes. It is rare for smallpox to spread through the air, but in confined spaces, it is possible. Johnson soon came down with smallpox and died. Whether or not he contracted the virus from Lincoln remains unconfirmed, but Johnson's proximity to the president during his illness suggests as much.

William Johnson, Essential Worker

William Johnson's job was essential to Lincoln's recovery. Then and now, essential workers are on the front lines during outbreaks of dangerous infectious diseases. Their jobs, like William Johnson's, increase their risk of exposure. Throughout history, these roles have been disproportionately filled by people from historically underrepresented groups, who die in greater numbers during outbreaks. Institutional racism makes it difficult, and in some cases impossible, for people from historically underrepresented groups to access the quality healthcare that is their human right.

CHAPTER 35

The Eradicators

By 1953, vaccines and public health laws—like mandatory vaccination—had eradicated smallpox in North America, Europe, and the islands of the Pacific Ocean, including Australia and New Zealand. Throughout the rest of the world, however, outbreaks of the disease continued taking lives each year.

At a 1958 meeting of the World Health Assembly (governing body of the World Health Organization [WHO], an agency of the United Nations), Russia's deputy minister of health, Dr. Viktor Zhdanov, proposed a global effort to eradicate smallpox. His proposal came during one of the most dangerous periods in world history. Known as the Cold War, it was an era of heightened political tension between the United States and Russia (then the Soviet Union), as the two superpower nations teetered on the edge of nuclear war. But in smallpox, even the world's two most powerful adversaries found a common goal: the global eradication of the disease. Zhdanov told the assembly that his country was willing to donate stockpiles of their vaccine for an eradication program. The assembly welcomed the Russians' proposal because it was the first time in nine years that the country had partici-pated. Accepting their offer to assist in a smallpox eradication program was good for public health and international diplo-macy. The assembly passed a resolution to eradicate smallpox worldwide.

Under the WHO's eradication plan, each country created a national campaign to carry out a mass vaccination program. The WHO further assisted in the program by developing facilities that produced vaccines for the international pro-gram. Mobile vaccination teams traveled throughout each country, village by village, in a coordinated effort to vaccinate the majority of their populations. The program's goal was to vaccinate 80 percent of people within three years, guided by a theory that an 80 percent vaccination rate would be enough to make most people in those communities immune to the disease—which is known as herd immunity.

However, by the mid-1960s, between 10 and 15 million cases of smallpox still occurred around the world each year, with one-third of those people dying even though a reliable vaccine was available. The WHO's eradication program had failed to permanently destroy the virus, and it remained endemic in thirty-three countries. A disease is endemic when it is constantly present in a given area, usually a state or country. Global health leaders and governments were frustrated because, of all known diseases, smallpox was an ideal candidate for eradication. It was easy to identify and confined to a single animal species: human beings. And while smallpox epidemics were deadly, they developed slowly, giving vaccinators time to intervene and halt the spread with shots.

In 1966, the WHO announced a new and "intensified" global smallpox eradication program, funded with money from the WHO's budget and supported by the CDC. The American agency recruited, trained, and deployed physicians and other healthcare advisors to assist with countries' vaccination campaigns. Each country established its own vaccination program, staffing teams with workers from that country.

Technology had advanced since the previous attempt at smallpox eradication. A freeze-dried version of the vaccine was easier to store, eliminating the need for refrigeration. A

new pressure-powered injector, the Ped-O-Jet, could deliver a thousand vaccines per hour.

It was eventually replaced by a much simpler tool, the bifurcated needle. Invented by Dr. Benjamin Rubin, the device did not have a syringe. It was a simple two-inch length of steel, resembling a shrimp fork with two tines at one end. The vaccinator dipped the needle into liquid vaccine to collect a single drop—the precise amount required for one dose. It was then injected into the arm through a series of shallow and relatively painless taps that lightly punctured the skin. The needles were small, portable, easy to sanitize, and inexpensive to manu-facture. With these new tools—as well as assistance from the CDC, and increased funding from the WHO—the goal of the intensi-fied eradication program was the elimination of smallpox everywhere on earth within ten years.

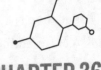

CHAPTER 36

Smallpox Hunter: William Foege

Yahe Township
Eastern Region of Nigeria

In March 1966, Dr. William "Bill" Foege accepted an assignment from the CDC to establish the WHO's newly intensified smallpox eradication plan in the eastern region of Nigeria. Foege was a former Epidemic Intelligence Service officer who had come to the country to run a small clinic and develop better public health infrastructure for the people who lived there. Foege and his colleague, David Thompson, also a former EIS officer, would be responsible for training and deploying teams of vaccinators throughout the region with the goal of vaccinating the entire population—what the WHO called mass vaccination. Trained vaccinators would carry out the vaccination of no less than 12 million people at a time when West and Central Africa had the highest rate of smallpox in the world.

By the end of that year, however, the WHO's mass vaccination strategy would be challenged in Nigeria, revolutionizing the way the global program addressed the eradication of smallpox.

On December 4, Foege and Thompson received a distress call over their radio—a missionary reporting an outbreak of smallpox in the village of Ovirpua. He wanted to know if the smallpox eradication team could help. Thompson and Foege grabbed their gear. Ovirpua was about a hundred miles away from their post in Yahe. Foege knew they would need reliable transportation to travel over the rugged terrain. A jeep wouldn't do; they needed something quicker and easy to maneuver. Foege and Thompson borrowed a couple of small French motorbikes that were light enough to carry—an added bonus when they ran out of road and would have to continue on foot.

By midday, they had arrived at Ovirpua. The first people they vaccinated were the families of the patients with smallpox, followed by anyone who had been in close contact with the sick. That night, by the glow of kerosene lamps, the disease detectives assessed the situation. The WHO's policy at the time was mass vaccination—that is, to vaccinate every eligible person in an area. But Foege and Thompson were running out of vaccine. They had no idea how much was required because they didn't know the size of the outbreak beyond Ovirpua.

An epidemiologist's response to an outbreak begins with surveillance. They must know where an outbreak is occurring before they can intervene to stop it. It's a strategy known as surveillance and containment, and it's the foundation of an epidemiologist's training. But Foege and Thompson didn't have any means of surveillance in the region. They didn't know if other villages were affected, where those villages were, how many people were sick, or for how long. They could not contact the other villages because there were no telephones. The only link to other villages was a network of shortwave radios operated by missionaries who were stationed across the country. Every night at 7:00 p.m. they turned on their radios and listened for any distress calls. Foege decided to use the shortwave radio network to conduct surveillance and find out if the virus was circulating elsewhere.

Foege radioed missionaries within thirty miles of Ovirpua and explained the situation. Using a map of the region, he divided the area into zones and assigned a missionary to each one. It was their job to send a runner to every village within their assigned zone to ask if there were any cases of smallpox. The next night, at 7:00 p.m., the shortwave radio in Ovirpua crackled to life as the missionaries reported their findings. Smallpox was present in just four villages, but Foege knew they did not have enough vaccine to carry out mass vaccinations. To maximize their limited quantity, Foege decided they would use it strategically to build a wall of immunity between people and the virus. It was a basic virus containment strategy known to epidemiologists as ring vaccination. If a person is exposed to a virus, they, as well as their close contacts, are vaccinated, creating a ring of immunity around the infected person, preventing the virus from spreading.

A virus is like a fire. If it has fuel in the form of hosts, it will continue to spread. Foege understood this fact better than most. Before he learned to fight deadly diseases, he learned how to fight forest fires. For two summers during his teenage years, he earned money for college by working with the US Forest Service in Washington and Oregon. During wildfires, one of Foege's jobs was to help construct a fire line. A group of eighteen to twenty firefighters would dig a trench around the perimeter of a fire, clearing brush and undergrowth until nothing remained but the soil. The trench became a natural barrier—a fire line—between the flames and their fuel source. Without access to fuel, the fire died.

Viruses operate on the same principle. Like a burning ember carried by the wind, a virus must eventually jump to a new host in order to survive. If a fire line dug into the dirt could stop a raging wildfire, could a fire line of immunization stop an outbreak of smallpox with a limited supply of vaccine? Foege believed it was possible.

"First we vaccinated the currently infected villages, where some people were probably already infected even if they had not yet developed symptoms," he wrote in his memoir. Vaccination would protect the recently infected against a severe case or perhaps prevent the disease altogether. "Those exposed even two weeks earlier would still get smallpox, but they would be surrounded by vaccinated people, making further transmission of the virus very difficult." Next, using information gathered from the network of missionaries,

Foege made educated guesses about other locations where the virus could be incubating, and then vaccinated those people as well.

Ring vaccination itself was not a revolutionary idea. But Foege's strategic use of ring vaccination to make the most of a limited vaccine supply was groundbreaking. And it worked! Ring vaccination halted the outbreak in the four villages using only a fraction of the supplies that would have been required to carry out a mass vaccination.

"If a house is on fire, no one wastes time pouring water on nearby houses just in case the fire spreads," Foege wrote. "They rush to pour water where it will do the most good— on the burning house. The same strategy turned out to be effective in eradicating smallpox."

From 1977 to 1983, Dr. Foege served as director of the CDC. In 2012, President Barack Obama awarded the veteran virus hunter the Presidential Medal of Freedom, America's highest civilian honor.

Bill Foege's ring vaccination strategy was eventually adopted throughout the smallpox eradication campaign, and the global coalition of virus hunters began pushing smallpox out of regions, countries, and eventually entire continents. In 1970, the number of affected countries shrank to eighteen. West Africa and South America were smallpox-free by 1971, followed by Afghanistan and Indonesia the next year. In 1973, smallpox was eliminated in Central and Southern Africa. However, it was still endemic in India. The large, densely populated country of over half a billion people had suffered repeated outbreaks of the disease for centuries and is widely believed to be smallpox's place of origin, where it is described in writings dating from 1500 BCE. The elimination of smallpox there was one of the biggest challenges facing the global eradication program.

CHAPTER 37

An Army of Virus Hunters

Initially, the government of India wanted to use the mass vaccination strategy. The WHO urged them to reconsider because mass vaccination in India was impractical. Twenty million babies were born every year—children who would also have to be vaccinated. WHO officials eventually convinced the country's leadership that finding every case of smallpox in the country and immediately surrounding those cases with a fire line of immunity using ring vaccination was far more effective. The smallpox virus would eventually be deprived of all viable hosts. With nowhere to replicate itself, variola would eventually die out.

To accomplish the overwhelming task of finding every last case of smallpox in India, the WHO partnered with the country's leadership to raise an army of 150,000 virus hunters. Beginning in 1973, they carried out surveillance and containment on a massive scale in the All-India Searches. One week per month, search teams across the country made house calls, visiting half a million villages and 150 million homes! Each eradication team worker carried a picture of a young boy with the disease. Over two billion copies of the photo were printed. Eradication workers showed the picture at each household, asking how many people lived in the home, and if anyone had smallpox. After completing all necessary vaccinations, workers recorded their results: the number of household members, the number of people vaccinated, and the number of people who still needed shots. This data was written on the exterior wall of the home using wet clay that dried like permanent ink. Future search teams would know the vaccination status of each person in that house. The search results were also meticulously recorded on paper and rapidly submitted to the program's leadership to track the progress of the searches. It's estimated that a single monthly search of every Indian household created eight tons of paperwork.

For the remainder of the month, the eradication teams fanned out into communities, visiting busy public places like schools, temples, and markets in search of smallpox. In the days leading up to a monthly search, the government of India publicized the eradication program. Flyers encouraging smallpox vaccination were printed and distributed. Radios, televisions, newspapers, and posters also announced a monetary reward of 100 rupees ($12 US) to anyone who reported a suspected case of smallpox. Prime Minister Indira Gandhi was personally involved in the publicity campaign. She sent messages to states with smallpox, urging people to get vaccinated.

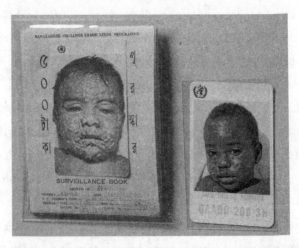

A smallpox eradication program worker's surveillance book, on display at the CDC David J. Sencer Museum in Atlanta, Georgia.

The use of the surveillance and containment strategy worked. By 1973, the eradication program had beaten back smallpox in four states in the southern part of India. Tamil Nadu, Kerala, Andhra Pradesh, and Karnataka were all smallpox-free. But the virus remained uncontrolled in the Indian states of Uttar Pradesh, Bihar, and West Bengal. Those three states were home to 189 million people. The WHO realized that outbreaks in those areas were not being detected early enough to intervene with vaccination. The eradication program needed better surveillance and more accurate reporting of cases to improve vaccinator response times and halt outbreaks sooner.

As the eradication effort zeroed in on the last regions to contain smallpox, a young American physician and CDC disease detective, Dr. Mary Guinan, prepared to join the fight.

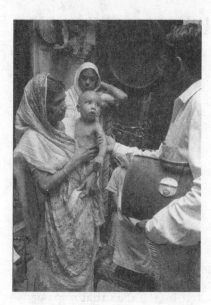

A doctor examines a child to find out if the child needs revaccination. New Delhi, India, 1963

CHAPTER 38

Smallpox Hunter: Mary Guinan

Atlanta, Georgia
Late 1974

Mary Guinan was an EIS officer at the CDC in Atlanta when she volunteered for the smallpox eradication program in India. "I was captivated by the idea that a group of idealists had laid out a plan to eradicate smallpox from the world," she wrote in her memoir. Humankind was on the brink of eliminating a disease for the first time in history, and Guinan was determined to be part of it. The global program was finally winning the war against smallpox in the country. Only two Indian states were still reporting cases, Uttar Pradesh and Bihar.

Every week the CDC issued a call for eradication program volunteers. Guinan had raised her hand twice and been rejected both times. She finally asked the director of the EIS, Dr. Philip Brachman, why she had not been accepted. Was it the CDC or the WHO refusing her offer to help? Brachman told her that India did not want to recruit women into the eradication program. Sexism was an all-too-familiar problem for Guinan, a woman who wanted to work in science, a field dominated by men.

Before she became a physician and a CDC disease detective, Guinan had tried to become an astronaut. In 1968, while completing her PhD in physiology, she took an aviation and space medicine course at NASA. In a class of approximately ten students, Guinan met every physical and medical prerequisite for the space program except one: she was a woman. At the time, women were restricted from entering NASA's Mission Control Center, for fear they would "distract the men."

Despite the disappointing setback, Guinan remained dedicated to a career in science that would serve others. She decided to become a doctor. But when she applied to medical schools, the rejection letters piled up. Like NASA, most universities favored male candidates. Guinan stubbornly refused to abandon her goal and, in 1972, graduated from the prestigious Johns Hopkins University School of Medicine.

Years later, she was still fighting against sexist attitudes as she tried to volunteer for the smallpox eradication program. Refusing to back down once again, Guinan reminded Dr. Brachman that the prime minister of India, Indira Gandhi, was a woman. Was she aware that qualified women who wanted to help India fight smallpox were being rejected based on their gender? Guinan asked Brachman if she could speak with the WHO or the Indian government to appeal the decision and he agreed to help.

A week later, Guinan's appeal was accepted, and she was invited to Uttar Pradesh, India, where she would devote herself to helping rid the world of smallpox for good.

In this 1991 photograph, Dr. Mary Guinan (left) shakes the hand of former US surgeon general Antonia C. Novello, the first woman and the first Hispanic to become surgeon general of the United States. Also pictured, former CDC director Dr. William L. Roper (1990–1993).

Uttar Pradesh, India
January 1975

When Mary Guinan arrived in India it was monsoon season, and the weather was taking a toll on the roads. Travel was difficult for her and her team, which included a driver and paramedical assistant, Shafi. Smallpox eradication teams were each assigned a territory where they would conduct surveillance and containment of smallpox using the ring vaccination strategy perfected by Bill Foege. "Our job was to . . . find persons infected with smallpox, immediately immunize all contacts of the patients, and then surround them with a [ten-mile] ring of immunity," Guinan wrote.

Equipped with supplies of vaccine, bifurcated needles, sleeping bags, and a jeep, Guinan and her team searched for smallpox through the muddy backcountry.

Their vehicle was no match for the deep ruts and potholes in the roads. And some villages were completely cut off, isolated from the mainland by deep rivers. It was crucial that she search every village for smallpox cases, so Guinan had to find a way across the water. Usually, she could arrange passage by boat, but they could be difficult to find. Sometimes she rented camels to cross rivers, but Guinan avoided them whenever possible. She had been bitten more than once by the sometimes unpredictable and aggressive animals.

Guinan and her team were only a month into their fieldwork when a solution to their transportation problem came racing toward them out of nowhere—literally. A black, dirt-covered Mercedes-Benz barreled down one of the more passable roads and screeched to a stop. A smiling, eager young man stepped out. The villagers called him Raj Sahib. He had heard that Guinan was part of the smallpox eradication effort and that crossing rivers to look for outbreaks had been a problem. He told Guinan he wanted to help. Sahib raised his hand and pointed down the road. Guinan looked

up to see an elephant and its driver, or mahout, making its
way toward them.

When Guinan confided that she had never ridden an
elephant, Raj Sahib suggested she give it a try. Guinan
hesitated, but if learning to ride an elephant would help
eradicate smallpox in India, she was willing to give the animal a chance.

The elephant lumbered over, and the mahout unfurled
a rickety nine-foot ladder from its back. Guinan carefully
stepped onto the first rung and began the unsteady climb.
When she reached the top, she took her seat on the animal's
massive back, settling into a big hemp-and-cloth-covered
saddle. Guinan immediately noticed the elephant's flesh was
unexpectedly pink in some places. She had never imagined
when she volunteered for the smallpox eradication program
that her work would include riding a pink elephant!

The animal eased into the river, swimming gracefully
through the deep water. To the delight of Raj Sahib, they
arrived safely on the other side. That day, Guinan's team
added two new members: the mahout and his elephant.

For three weeks, "the elephant was a dream addition to
the team," Guinan recalled. At the end of each day, the elephant and mahout left, but returned the next morning. The
animal made it easier to traverse rivers in search of smallpox,
which enabled Guinan and her team to complete their fieldwork ahead of schedule.

In April, Guinan departed Uttar Pradesh, India, to return
to her job in Atlanta as an EIS officer. The following month,

the WHO announced that Uttar Pradesh was smallpox-free. By July 1975, Bihar, which had been the last remaining Indian state with reported cases, would also be declared free of smallpox.

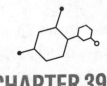

CHAPTER 39

Smallpox Hunter: Cornelia Davis

West Bengal, India
July 1975

Dr. Cornelia "Connie" Davis plopped down under a sad little tree. It looked as dismal as she felt. That morning, she and her team, which included a driver, Abdul; and Dinesh, a medical assistant, had stopped at a nearby village and discovered that India's eradication hopes could be in jeopardy. A local man told her he had heard about rash and fever cases across the border, in Bangladesh. Davis's assigned territory in the Indian state of West Bengal was close to the country's border. If the suspicious cases in Bangladesh turned out to be smallpox, the disease could reenter India, sparking another large-scale outbreak. It was the worst kind of news at the worst possible time. India was preparing to announce that smallpox had been eliminated

in the country. It was up to Davis and her team to prevent any new smallpox cases from crossing the Indian border, where the virus could regain a foothold.

As a young doctor, Connie Davis had been ecstatic when she received the invitation to help eradicate smallpox in India. D. A. Henderson, chief medical officer of the WHO eradication program, warned that conditions would be unpredictable, uncomfortable, even dangerous. But Davis wasn't intimidated by rugged conditions and terrain. She had been a Girl Scout, earning the organization's highest honor, known at the time as the Curved Bar. During summer breaks from college, she'd led scouts on fifty-mile backpacking trips into the rugged Colorado wilderness. Once, a camper cut herself and was hemorrhaging blood, and Davis had to map the quickest way out of the wilderness to get help. She recalled how frightened she had been at the time, "but once I focused on the here and now," she said, "the panic gave way. I always calmed down once I focused."

As she sat beneath the decrepit tree, Davis imagined the scathing criticism she could face if she failed to prevent new cases of smallpox from being imported back into India, where no new cases had been reported since May 24. "I could just hear the discussion," she wrote years later. "*You send a woman epidemiologist to do a job, and she [messes] up! Not only that, but she's a [B]lack woman and an American.*" Davis wrenched her attention from those painful thoughts and focused on the problem. She felt the anxiety subside. Smallpox would not be allowed to reenter India, she decided. Not on her team's watch.

Davis considered the facts. If word of possible smallpox cases in Bangladesh had already reached this man in India, it was logical that the affected village was close to the border. She could simply cross from India into Bangladesh, visit the village, and verify if the rash and fever cases were smallpox.

But crossing an international border was strictly forbidden by the WHO. An eradication worker could not stray from their assigned country. Still, Davis's instincts were telling her that the cases in Bangladesh were smallpox. If the village was close to the border as she suspected, perhaps she could get in quickly, confirm a smallpox diagnosis, and get back out undetected.

Dr. Connie Davis delivers a presentation to a group of smallpox eradication program colleagues, 1977.

"Willingness to serve is not enough," according to the Girl Scout Handbook. A scout must also "know how to do the job well, even in an emergency." Davis believed that preventing smallpox from reentering India constituted an emergency, and in order to do her job well, she would have to break the rules.

After concealing their jeep in the bushes, the three disease detectives set off along a narrow pathway lined with rice and jute fields. When they first crossed the border into Bangladesh, Davis, Dinesh, and Abdul were completely alone. Davis was uneasy. She didn't have a map to guide them. All she knew for certain was that they were in Bangladesh, headed south.

About two miles down the trail, they intersected with a busy crossroads, bustling with people and wagons. Dinesh asked around about the possible outbreak and learned that the village in question was west of their current location. The team hopped in the back of a wagon and set off toward the village. Forty minutes later, they arrived.

"An older man was brought to us right away," Davis recalled. "We introduced ourselves, and I told him we had heard rumors that they had rash-and-fever cases and we were wondering if it was smallpox." As Dinesh translated, Davis learned that the man's entire family was sick. He led the team to his hut.

They found two adults and six children, all with cases of smallpox. It was the first time Davis had seen a case of the disease in person. Needing more information to determine the extent of the outbreak, she asked if anyone in their family had traveled into India. If so, cases could already be incubating on their side of the border. The family assured her that they had not crossed into India and that no one had visited them since they became sick. At that point, there were no other known cases in the village, but Davis knew surveillance and containment measures in the area needed to begin immediately. But Davis's team couldn't do it. They weren't supposed to be there in the first place. She would have to contact the WHO and make sure smallpox eradication workers in Bangladesh were notified of the outbreak. Davis and her team had done as much as they could. It would be up to Bangladesh's eradication team to finish the job.

By midday, the trio was back in India. With a smallpox outbreak confirmed so close to the border, Davis requested more help to search three nearby Indian villages to ensure that there were no cases of smallpox. Next, she sent a telegram to WHO headquarters stating that she had found smallpox cases in Bangladesh and that she was beginning containment procedures on India's side of the border as a precautionary measure. Davis accepted that after the WHO officials received her telegram, they would know she had disobeyed the rules by crossing the border into Bangladesh. Still, she believed that she had made the right decision, no matter the consequences.

Several days later, Davis received word that containment activities were underway in the Bangladeshi village where she had discovered the outbreak. Her fear of a reprimand because of the unapproved border crossing was never realized. Quite the opposite, in fact: Davis was eventually promoted to a surveillance post over the entire Indian state of Rajasthan, where she continued her meticulous work, monitoring the region for smallpox outbreaks for another eighteen months.

After July 1975, there was no evidence of smallpox *anywhere* in the country.

Smallpox Zero

By late autumn of 1975, there had not been a single reported case of smallpox in Bangladesh for two months. Then toddler Rahima Banu fell ill with the disease. She and her family were quickly vaccinated and isolated themselves at home until the child was no longer contagious. Meanwhile, the 18,000 people who lived within a 1.5-mile radius of the Banus' home were vaccinated as well. For at least a month, smallpox eradication workers combed the area, searching for any sign of infection in others. They found none. Rahima survived, and hers was the last known case of naturally occurring smallpox on the Indian subcontinent.

During the next two years, smallpox surveillance continued in India as a safety precaution, but the virus did not reemerge. With so much immunity in the population from the vaccination campaigns, the virus died out.

In 1977, the world's last remaining known case of endemic smallpox was contained in Somalia. At that point, there were no other known cases of the disease anywhere in the world.

On May 8, 1980, the Thirty-Third World Health Assembly made a formal resolution officially declaring that smallpox had been eradicated worldwide. To date, there have been no other naturally occurring cases anywhere. It was a historic achievement in global public health.

"Smallpox is Dead!" Front cover of the magazine of the World Health Organization. "World Health" (May 1980). Design by Peter Davies.

CHAPTER 40
The Legacy of Smallpox

Many of the names of those who helped eradicate smallpox are well-known in the field of epidemiology. But humankind owes the greatest debt to hundreds of thousands of Indigenous public health workers around the world, whose names will never be known. They partnered with the WHO eradication workers to carry out the boots-on-the-ground shoe-leather epidemiology required to contain every single case of smallpox on Earth. Through an extraordinary global effort, a deadly disease was eradicated for the first (and for now, the only) time in history. To credit this feat to a single person or select group of individuals is to ignore the most crucial element of the smallpox eradication program: teamwork. It was groups of people of all nationalities working together for the common good that made eradication possible. Science can provide the tools, but it is shared humanity and the willingness to help that compels people to overcome impossible odds in order to care for one another.

Bill Foege cautions, however, that it's easy to forget to be grateful for the fact that we no longer have to live in a world where this deadly, disfiguring disease exists. "People rarely reflect on the fact that they have not had to deal with smallpox, tuberculosis, whooping cough, diphtheria, rabies, or other controlled maladies in their lifetimes," he wrote in his memoir. "Yet this is not by chance. Every disease encounter missed is the result of deliberate actions taken by unknown benefactors in the past."

Today, live variola virus exists in only two secured laboratories: the Centers for Disease Control and Prevention in Atlanta, Georgia, and the State Research Center of Virology and Biotechnology (VECTOR Institute) in Koltsovo, Russia. The decision to keep any stores of the virus after its eradication was controversial. Opponents of the decision argued that maintaining any smallpox supply was dangerous because it could be weaponized. However, others believed that there was more to gain by studying the variola virus. Since eradication, scientists have used it to develop better vaccines, drug therapies, and diagnostic tests for smallpox in the unlikely event that it reemerges. These therapies also treat other types of poxviruses, including mpox.

In May of 2022, this less virulent cousin of smallpox caused a global outbreak. As of December 27, 2023, there have been more than 92,000 reported cases worldwide and

170 confirmed deaths. The disease was first discovered in 1959 when a monkey in a Danish laboratory broke out in bodily sores that resembled smallpox. The new zoonotic virus was named for the primate species in which it was first identified, but it's now believed that the virus's natural host is rodents.

The smallpox vaccine was effective in preventing mpox. But after the worldwide eradication of smallpox, the vaccine campaigns ended. Communities in parts of Africa where the disease remains endemic were left vulnerable to mpox outbreaks.

Disease detective Dr. Neil Vora, whose father survived smallpox as a child in India, stresses that health inequity is at the heart of the recent mpox epidemic. "The [mpox] situation is a real tragedy," he says. "This is a virus we have known about for years. We have a vaccine for it. We have a therapeutic for it. We know that the virus causes illness in Africa . . . in recent years, an ongoing outbreak in Nigeria . . . Yet African infected areas were not given access to a vaccine."

Dr. Vora warns that even the most prepared people can be caught off guard when an outbreak occurs. Scientists and governments must be willing to share lifesaving vaccines and medicines with poorer countries, he says, because "infectious diseases can pack surprises that no amount of preparation will be sufficient for."

The eradication of smallpox contributed to a growing belief in the medical community that science could prevent or control almost any infection. What no one could have known at the time, however, was that a new zoonotic virus had jumped from a chimpanzee into a human sometime in the nineteenth century. The deadly infection, which we now know as HIV/AIDS, had been spreading around the world, undetected, until it was first identified in Los Angeles and New York City in 1981, shortly after the victory against smallpox was announced. The discovery of the new virus shattered the faith of those scientists who had been bold enough to believe humankind had finally won the war against infectious disease.

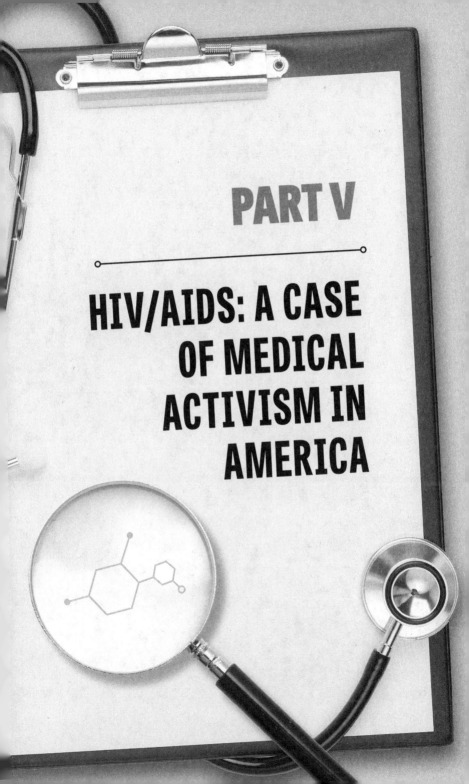

PART V

HIV/AIDS: A CASE OF MEDICAL ACTIVISM IN AMERICA

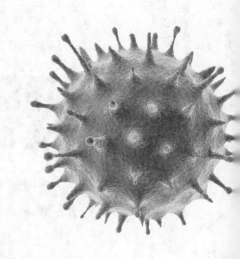

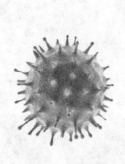

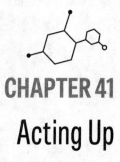

CHAPTER 41

Acting Up

he piercing cry of an air horn split the silence as hundreds of unarmed activists marched onto the campus of the National Institutes of Health (NIH) in Bethesda, Maryland. They paraded across the perfectly manicured lawns, stabbing signs into the air. Protest chants reverberated off the brick walls of the elite scientific research facility: "Act up! Fight back! Fight AIDS!" "Act up! Fight back! Fight AIDS!"

The elaborate demonstration was a spectacle of civil disobedience: theatrical costumes, makeup and masks, even special effects. Rainbow-colored smoke billowed from twenty-foot poles and wafted by the institution's windows, where scientists and researchers gathered to watch. The activists were protesting government scientists at the NIH, whom

Activists descended on the National Institutes of Health to protest the government's failure to adequately address the AIDS crisis in America.

they believed were responsible for the deaths of thousands of people from HIV/AIDS.

President Ronald Reagan had largely ignored the deadly epidemic because HIV/AIDS was initially observed in gay men, an already stigmatized community of people. Reagan had been elected in 1981, six months before the first AIDS cases were reported in Los Angeles. It wasn't until four years later that he finally mentioned AIDS publicly for the first time. Responding to a reporter's question about his administration's inadequate response to the outbreak, Reagan called AIDS a "top priority," despite all evidence to the contrary. By the summer of 1985, at least 12,000 cases had been reported in the US and nearly 6,000 people had died.

In New York City, battle lines were drawn—the United

States government on one side, and people with HIV/AIDS and their allies on the other. Among them was activist and author Larry Kramer. In March 1987, he announced the formation of an organization that would fight for the rights of people with AIDS. The AIDS Coalition to Unleash Power—or ACT UP—was born. The organization's members came from every walk of life, some wealthy, some poor. They were artists, actors, authors, bankers, musicians, filmmakers, playwrights, singers, stock traders. They quickly learned how to make the most of the group's collective talent, imagination, and intellect, and ACT UP grew into a global force for change with thousands of members, becoming one of the most influential activist groups in American history.

On the NIH campus, more wailing air horns erupted at twelve-minute intervals. It was a memorial. In the US—despite it being the wealthiest country in the world and home to some of the best doctors, scientists, and researchers—a person died of AIDS every twelve minutes. By the end of 1990, there would be over 160,000 reported cases in the US and more than 120,000 deaths. As the loud but nonviolent protest continued, law enforcement officers moved in to control the crowd. Mounted police used their horses like battering rams, shoving the animals into the activists' bodies in an attempt to corral the demonstration. In a disturbing video of the protest, one of those mounted officers can be seen clubbing a peaceful protestor with his baton.

A defiant protester stares down a mounted police officer during the May 1990 protest at the NIH in Bethesda, Maryland.

The demonstration continued, the activists marching, chanting, and calling out one particular scientist by name, over and over again— Dr. Anthony Fauci, the director of the National Institute of Allergy and Infectious Diseases. The NIAID was one of the twenty-seven institutes and centers that made up the National Institutes of Health, where Fauci was the lead government scientist in charge of HIV/AIDS research. "Dr. Anthony Fauci is deciding the research priorities for the National Institutes of Allergy and Infectious Diseases," activist Garance Franke-Ruta said during the May 21 protest. "We want them to stop the secret meetings . . . and we want people from affected communities to have voting power and speaking power because [the scientists] are not going to get anywhere against [HIV/AIDS] until they're actively dealing with the people who are most affected by the disease." ACT UP believed that people with HIV/AIDS and their allies deserved a seat on the committees that made decisions about the government's clinical drug trials. They demanded equality within the trials as well. The Center for Disease Control and Prevention's (CDC) original case definition of AIDS was based on the experience of gay men. As a result, women with HIV/AIDS who presented with symptoms or infections not covered by the case definition were unable to receive adequate medical care. Sixty-five percent of women who were HIV-positive died having never been properly diagnosed with AIDS. Race and poverty were also barriers to treatment. AIDS would eventually become "the third leading cause of death among Black men and women between the ages of 35 and 44, and the fourth leading cause of death among Latinos of the same age group."

In the midst of the protest, a young activist with wavy brown hair, a lean build, and a backpack made his move. Out of sight of law enforcement, twenty-nine-year-old Peter Staley scampered onto a low-level roof of the NIAID. Once he was in position, he quickly pulled a banner from his backpack and taped it to the front of the building. The words *SILENCE = DEATH* were printed on a black background beneath the base of a pink triangle, the ACT UP logo.

Staley's presence on the roof was quickly interrupted by the police who had noticed his stunt and clambered onto the roof after him. Down below, his fellow ACT UPers screamed their disapproval, chanting, "The whole world is watching! The whole world is watching!" as their comrade was lowered to the ground.

The police handcuffed Staley and placed him under arrest. As the cops marched him through the building toward a waiting police van, a man wearing a crisp white lab coat appeared, striding confidently toward the scene. In a voice brimming with genuine concern, he called out, "Peter, are you all right?" The police detaining the young activist stopped cold. The man in the lab coat was Dr. Anthony Fauci, director of the NIAID—the person being loudly and angrily condemned by the crowd outside. Some of them carried signs calling Fauci a murderer. And yet the doctor appeared genuinely worried about this particular activist, whose name he seemed to know. The officers were confused, and Staley began to laugh. "I'm fine," he replied to Fauci. "Just doing my job. How about you, Tony?"

CHAPTER 42

The Activist

Peter Staley had been just twenty-four years old when his doctor gave him the news. He had a condition called ARC—AIDS-related complex. The term is not used today, but early in the AIDS epidemic it described a person with HIV who exhibited relatively mild symptoms. Mild or not, Staley was sick with a life-threatening illness. It was 1985, and there was no effective treatment or cure for the human immunodeficiency virus.

HIV is like a smart bomb that strikes the body's strategic defense force, the immune system. The virus targets the CD4, or helper T cells, hacking their machinery in order to make more copies of itself. Eventually the infected cell dies and the virus spreads to other living cells. When the body no longer manufactures enough helper T cells, the amount of virus in the body increases. T cells fall to dangerously low levels and the body is more vulnerable to infections. People don't die of AIDS; they die of AIDS-related illnesses. Staley had gone to the doctor for nothing more than a nagging cough, but it had turned his life upside down.

As a kid, Peter Staley had dreamed of a life as a concert pianist. But during college, he changed his major from music to finance and spent a semester abroad, studying at the world-renowned London School of Economics. During those first years after graduating, before his diagnosis, Staley's life had unfolded just as he'd hoped. He had a boyfriend he adored and a promising career. Following in his older brother's foot-steps, he had landed a job as a bond trader for J.P. Morgan. The work was thrilling, if stressful, and Staley was good at it.

Two years after his diagnosis, however, Staley's body was struggling to keep up with the demands of his job. He began a course of AZT, an experimental drug approved by the FDA in March 1987. It was the only drug available to treat HIV/AIDS at the time, but it was toxic. Staley, like half the people who tried AZT, could not tolerate it. He was exhausted all the time and nodding off at his trading desk. No one at work knew he was ill—or that he was gay. He'd heard the homo-phobic slurs his colleagues carelessly tossed around. He could never trust them with the truth about who he was.

One morning as he was walking to work, a young man on the street handed him a flyer for an ACT UP protest. Staley realized that the activists were fearlessly speaking out on behalf of people living with HIV/AIDS—people just like him. The following Monday, Staley attended his first ACT UP meeting.

A year later, Staley was too sick to continue working. He didn't know how long he had to live, but he decided that he would spend whatever time he had left standing shoulder to shoulder with his fellow activists. He would use his voice to defend people with HIV/AIDS against the government and pharmaceutical companies, and their scientists.

The scientist at the top of ACT UP's list was Dr. Anthony Fauci.

CHAPTER 43

The Scientist

Dr. Fauci had been on the front lines in the fight against HIV/AIDS since the virus was first detected. On June 5, 1981, he was in his office at the National Institute of Allergy and Infectious Diseases, scanning the CDC's *Morbidity and Mortality Weekly Report*. Beneath an article about dengue fever, there was one titled "*Pneumocystis* Pneumonia—Los Angeles." Fauci began to read. "In the period October 1980 [to] May 1981, five young men, all active homosexuals, were treated for biopsy-confirmed *Pneumocystis carinii* pneumonia." According to the article, two of the patients had died. "Being a busy young investigator at the time," Fauci recalled, "I put it in my desk and said, this must be a fluke. It's going to go away."

Since Fauci arrived at the NIH in 1968 at the age of

twenty-seven, his heavy workload and dedication to research had yielded impressive results. He was studying vasculitis, a disorder that causes inflammation of the blood vessels. When Fauci began studying a rare form of vasculitis (Wegener's granulomatosis) the disease was usually fatal. A breakthrough came when he was called to consult with doctors at the National Cancer Institute. The physicians were struggling to help patients whose immune systems were being suppressed by the powerful and toxic drugs used in chemotherapy treatments. The medication was making them more susceptible to infections. That gave Fauci an idea. If doses of powerful and toxic chemotherapy drugs caused an underreaction of the immune system in a cancer patient, perhaps small doses of the high-powered chemotherapy drug would *prevent an*

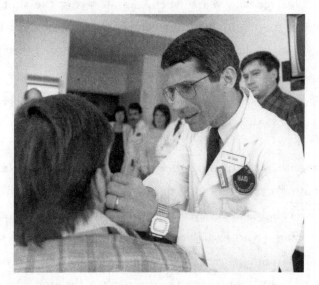

Dr. Anthony Fauci examines a person with HIV/AIDS, 1987.

overreaction of the immune systems in people with vasculitis. When Fauci and his colleagues tested the treatment in their vasculitis patients, the death rate dropped from 100 percent to 7 percent. Fauci's discovery had, in essence, cured the rare form of the disease.

Anthony Fauci grew up in the tough-as-nails Bensonhurst neighborhood of Brooklyn, New York. The son of a pharmacist, Fauci and his family lived above his father's drugstore. It was a true family business in which everyone, including Anthony, his sister, and his mother, all worked the cash register. After Anthony learned how to ride a bicycle, he made deliveries to his father's customers.

Fauci's confidence and natural leadership skills were evident in his teenage years when, despite being the shortest person on the team, Tony was named captain of the Regis High School basketball squad. It was during those formative years that Fauci also realized he wanted to use his life and talents to serve others. "It's what drove me to go to medical school," he said.

One month after reading the article reporting the unusual pneumonia cases in Los Angeles, a second article in the *MMWR* caught Fauci's eye. It described twenty-six patients—all gay men—who had *Pneumocystis* pneumonia as well as Kaposi's sarcoma, a rare skin cancer normally found in older Mediterranean men that can occur when the immune system is severely compromised. Fauci realized the article from the previous month had not been a fluke after all. *Oh my God*, he thought. *This is a brand-new disease*. "I actually got goosebumps," he said. It was a turning point in Fauci's career. He immediately began transitioning his laboratory to focus on the study of the new disease reported by the CDC. By the end of the following year, Fauci was seeing patients suffering from the disease in his clinic, while also studying it in the laboratory.

Not all of Fauci's colleagues were supportive of his choice. "Some people, I remember, were a little—I would say—concerned about me," he said. They did not understand why he was so eager to pivot from research in which he was an expert to a new disease that he knew nothing about. "But the fact was," Fauci said, "nobody was an expert yet." He believed the world was on the edge of a potentially catastrophic outbreak. "It was clear to me that this disease would turn out to be a major public health problem," he said, because "it wasn't restricted to just gay men." The illness was blood-borne and sexually transmitted, meaning any person could get it from a sexual partner or a blood transfusion. Injection drug users could get it by sharing contaminated needles, and pregnant women with HIV could transmit the infection to their unborn babies. In 1982, the new disease became known as Acquired Immune Deficiency Syndrome (AIDS). The following year, there were 1,450 reported cases in the US. It was this type of challenge that had driven Fauci to pursue a career in medicine. He had always wanted to make a big impact on the lives of his patients, and that desire attracted him to serious, life-threatening diseases. "I wanted to be where the action was," he said. Being "where the action was," however, came at a high price. Despite Fauci's efforts, the patients in his clinic continued to die. "Every once in a while, when you're involved in a difficult situation you get bad news . . ." Fauci said, recalling those early years of the AIDS crisis. "And then sometimes encouraging news comes along to make you feel a little better." But in those days, he said, "It was all bad."

There was nothing doctors could do, Fauci recalled. "It was just so unbelievably frustrating when you're used to being able to fix things and you're just not fixing anything," he said. Fauci watched helplessly for years as, one after another, his patients died.

CHAPTER 44

"A Working Confrontation"

Fauci had been a regular target of ACT UP demonstrations since the organization formed in 1987. At first, he was shocked to be singled out. For years, he had been working night and day trying to help people with AIDS, only to be called a murderer. But then, Fauci says, something shifted within him. He realized that he had never imagined what it must be like for people with HIV/AIDS, fearing for their own lives and the lives of the people they loved. "I decided that I would be doing exactly what they were doing," he said. Rather than ignore the activists like so many of his colleagues, he would sit down with them and listen to their concerns. Not long after ACT UP was founded in 1987, Fauci began to meet with members of the organization.

In October of 1989, ACT UP invited Dr. Fauci to one of

their meetings at the Lesbian and Gay Community Center (now known as the Lesbian, Gay, Bisexual & Transgender Community Center) in New York. They called it "a working confrontation." The meeting "was the first and only time in ACT UP's early history where anybody in government came to us," Peter Staley recalled. With over a hundred activists in the room, Fauci hoped to answer questions, describe the government's position on HIV/AIDS research, and find some common ground. But the crowd was understandably hostile. They didn't trust Fauci. He was the face of the government that had been largely ignoring the crisis since the beginning of the epidemic in 1981. Some members of the crowd jeered and hurled accusations. Fauci listened quietly as they blamed him for the deaths of their loved ones and friends, and he did not turn away. Rather than reject their criticism of the government's handling of the AIDS crisis, Fauci took responsibility for it. But as ACT UP member David Barr recalled, "The criticism, the hostility, it didn't really seem to faze him." Tony Fauci, the tough kid from Bensonhurst, didn't cower in the face of so much vitriol, nor did he lash out or leave. Peter Staley was impressed. "He got a complete grilling and continued the conversation," he said. Dr. Fauci was more than just another scientist in a suit. He did not hide behind his job title or a laboratory bench. He did something few other government scientists were willing to do at the time— he listened. Some of the activists continued to label Fauci as their enemy, but for Peter Staley, it was more complicated than that. "I couldn't shake the feeling that as the head of our government's AIDS research efforts, Dr. Fauci had my life in his hands."

As Fauci listened to the activists' concerns, he was impressed by the depth of knowledge in the room. Many of them asked well-informed, science-based questions. Although most were not trained scientists, some of the activists had read medical textbooks and papers published in scientific journals. "[The activists] elevated themselves by their own self-education about these things," Fauci said. "It became very, very clear that you weren't gonna mess with these people because they knew exactly what you were talking about and they knew exactly what they were talking about." Fauci and the activists didn't "agree on everything," he recalled, "but [the activists'] instincts were right."

Fauci was also beginning to realize that the activists had a point. The rules governing clinical trials were too strict. "The way we approached clinical trials had a degree of rigidity," he said. "Some flexibility was needed." But there were limits. "You cannot just cave in and let people tell you how to do science the wrong way," he insisted, "but there is a lot you can learn from understanding how the disease is affecting a particular population." The more he learned about the activists, the more Fauci believed that the people most affected by the AIDS crisis deserved to be part of the scientific process to develop and test the drugs that could save their lives. It was a revolutionary idea in clinical medicine at a time when not everyone wanted a revolution. Some of Fauci's scientific colleagues at the NIH and in other government branches believed he was wrong to directly engage with the activist community. They feared that allowing input from people who were not trained scientists set a dangerous precedent that would hamper research efforts. It was another crossroads in Fauci's career. Colleagues had questioned his judgment when he pivoted to the study of AIDS in 1981. Now, years later, he was defying expectations again because he believed that engaging with the activists was the moral thing to do. Fauci's actions demonstrated his belief that protecting public health involved more than what could be measured in a clinical trial.

Fauci had established common ground with some of the ACT UP members, but people were still dying of AIDS. As much as Peter Staley and other activists respected him, their fight against Fauci and the government was just getting started.

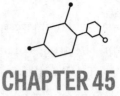

CHAPTER 45

Comfort and Community

According to activist and ACT UP member Jim Eigo, word spread quickly that the organization was trying to help people with AIDS, offering them a place to find comfort and community. "On Monday nights ACT UP gave a home to people who were sick, people who were not yet sick, and to their friends, and people who cared for them," he said. Before long, the meetings were standing-room-only events with 400 or more people in attendance. When there were not enough folding chairs for everyone, ACT UPers leaned against the white iron poles that jutted from the floor of the community center.

Members were encouraged to share ideas with the group and suggest ways to collaborate or channel their talents and enthusiasm into action. When five or more people shared a particular interest, they formed an "affinity group." These private groups of up to twenty activists were part of the larger ACT UP collective, each with their own identities. Affinity groups might hold separate meetings in someone's home to plan protest actions based on their shared interest. When a member was dying, affinity groups sometimes became caregiving groups for that person.

At large protests, affinity groups staged their own actions designed to attract media attention. Peter Staley called the results "a twelve-ring circus of powerful made-for-TV moments."

ACT UP members also formed committees. Open to all activists, these public groups reported to the Monday-night meetings and focused on specific areas such as media, fundraising, and healthcare access. The Treatment and Data Committee (T&D) was an unapologetically nerdy bunch that dove headfirst into the deep end of HIV/AIDS research. "The latest science or treatment would be discussed literally down to its molecular level," Peter Staley wrote. Then the committee condensed what they learned into a weekly digest that they distributed among the activists. T&D also hosted teach-ins to explain scientific research and technical jargon to ACT UP members so that every activist had an opportunity to learn about the work that scientists were doing to fight AIDS.

Not every member of ACT UP was on a committee, or a prominent figure in front of the cameras. Sarah Schulman was a rank-and-file member of the organization. It was activists like Schulman who turned out in large numbers to make the protests impossible to ignore. Schulman was also one of the first journalists to write about the government's failed response to the AIDS crisis. She eventually cofounded the ACT UP Oral History Project to document and preserve the legacy of the group's fight for health justice.

As ACT UP New York grew, their message spread across the country. Other US cities founded ACT UP chapters, setting the stage for a massive protest that would be the organization's first national demonstration.

CHAPTER 46

"ACT UP's National Coming Out"

The protest in front of the Food and Drug Administration (FDA) in Rockville, Maryland, was scheduled for October 11, 1988. One month before, the Treatment and Data Committee offered the FDA a chance to prevent the protest. They requested a meeting with the head of the agency, Commissioner Frank Young. T&D wanted to negotiate. If an agreement could be reached, the protest would be canceled. Young agreed to meet with members of the committee at FDA headquarters and hear their list of demands.

The group told Young that ACT UP wanted the clinical drug trials to be more humane. AZT was the only drug approved by the FDA to treat HIV/AIDS, but the activists condemned the methods used to test the drug in trials, calling them unethical. The AZT clinical trial had been a placebo-controlled study in which some participants received a placebo, or sugar pill, instead of the actual drug. The activists argued that it was cruel to withhold a drug from a trial participant if it could potentially extend their life. They wanted the FDA to stop using placebos in future HIV drug trials.

Drugs should also be available, the activists told Young, as soon as they "appear[ed] safe and at least theoretically effective." Finally, they demanded that the FDA do a better job of monitoring the pharmaceutical companies that were developing drugs to fight AIDS. ACT UP wanted the FDA to force those companies to disclose their financial information to prevent price gouging. When Burroughs Wellcome, the company that developed AZT, first released the drug in 1987, it was the only medication approved by the FDA for the treatment of HIV. At that point, it was the highest-priced drug in US history, costing $10,000 per year. Many people with HIV/AIDS could not afford the expensive medication. Young listened to the activists' list of demands but did not agree to any of them. The protest was on.

More than a thousand protestors from fifty ACT UP groups around the US converged on FDA headquarters in Maryland. They marched, chanted, and stared down the police in a protest that lasted hours. At a nearby podium, film historian, author, and ACT UP member Vito Russo addressed the crowd.

"I'm here today because I don't want to die. I know that there are eighty drugs that haven't been tested yet by the

FDA. I want to know why it takes five to ten years in this country to test drugs that you can test in Europe in a third of the time. We are simply asking the FDA to do it quicker."

Russo's speech and the FDA protest became a national news story thanks to ACT UP's media team. Ann Northrop, a former TV news producer, helped devise a brilliant and innovative media strategy. The protest organizers located as many ACT UP activists from as many different states as possible to serve as media spokespeople. They formed a line next to the podium, each person holding a sign with the name of their state written on it. After Russo's speech, the media was invited to address their questions to the newly deputized group of media representatives. "Go find someone from your home state to tell their personal story to your readers from your hometown," ACT UP media team members told the press, "and connect all of this locally." The journalists swarmed the line of sign holders for interviews. "And that is how we ended up not only all over the national news," Northrop said, "but in all these hometown papers all over the country because we had planned . . . to supply them with their local people."

News of the protest was printed and broadcast across the country and around the world. "We made the front page in Boston, Baltimore, Dallas, Houston, Orlando, and Miami," ACT UP member Mark Harrington wrote, "and were well-covered in Atlanta, Buffalo, Chicago, Detroit, Los Angeles, Memphis, New York, Philadelphia, San Francisco, St. Louis, Tampa, Tucson, and Washington, DC." The FDA protest,

Peter Staley said, was "ACT UP's big, national coming out." The national AIDS movement had begun.

Peter Staley attends an ACT UP meeting.

CHAPTER 47

A Case for Compassion

After ACT UP's national protest, it took just five months for the FDA to take action on one of the group's most important demands: the faster approval of experimental drugs.

An antiviral medication called ganciclovir, first developed in 1984, was the only known treatment for cytomegalovirus (CMV). The infection was common in people with AIDS and the suspected cause of death for one-third of patients. CMV could cause severe pneumonia, diarrhea, and lesions on the brain. When it attacked the retina and optical nerve, CMV caused blindness.

Ganciclovir had never been officially approved by the FDA. Two rival pharmaceutical companies, Syntex and Burroughs Wellcome, had separately but simultaneously developed the same drug in 1984, leading to a patent dispute.

Until it was settled, neither company could perform the necessary controlled studies of the drug. In the meantime, the FDA's compassionate use rule allowed doctors to request special authorization to administer a not-yet-fully-approved drug—in this case, ganciclovir—to qualifying patients with advanced illness. For two years, many doctors successfully treated their CMV patients with the drug under the compassionate use rule. When ganciclovir was administered in time, their eyesight could be saved. Doctors who prescribed the medication began reporting that the overall health of their patients on the drug was improving as well. Some doctors stated that the use of ganciclovir was actually prolonging the lives of people with CMV.

By 1986, Syntex had won the patent dispute and asked the FDA for its approval to market ganciclovir. However, the company's only data proving the drug's efficacy and safety came from the compassionate use cases. That was not good enough for the FDA. The application was rejected because the agency's policy stated that data from a controlled study was required for drug approval.

But due to the patent issue, those formal trials had never been completed by Syntex. In order to earn FDA approval, the company complied with the policy and agreed to a controlled study of ganciclovir. But the Syntex bid for FDA approval had potentially devastating consequences for people with AIDS who needed the drug. The agency introduced new criteria for patients in the ganciclovir trial, complicating—and limiting—some patients' access to the medication. The fact that ganciclovir had been safely and effectively treating CMV for years didn't matter. The FDA was handcuffed by its own rigid rules and regulations.

The controversy was precisely why ACT UP demanded changes in the way the FDA approved drugs. Any clinical trial that limited access to a medication—especially one with a proven track record—was inhumane, they argued. Many doctors who treated people with AIDS agreed. One called the study "mean."

A representative group from ACT UP went to visit Dr. Fauci at his office. They wanted him to persuade FDA commissioner Frank Young that the trial was cruel and unfair. Fauci agreed that government red tape was condemning people who were already suffering. He had witnessed the devastation of cytomegalovirus firsthand.

One of Fauci's patients with CMV had been a young man whose vision was deteriorating. Fauci knew the patient's prognosis was eventual blindness. Years later, Fauci recalled how kind this particular patient had been, and how friendly, often complimenting Dr. Fauci on his smile. One day, Fauci walked into the patient's room and before the doctor spoke, the man asked, "Who's there?" Dr. Fauci was devastated. "It was clear that he had gone completely blind," he said.

After meeting with the activists, Fauci publicly announced that he believed ganciclovir should be made available to everyone during the clinical trial. "I think it's the right thing to do, both ethically and medically," he told the *New York Times*. It was a message that Fauci also delivered to the US

Congress when he testified that he believed the drug was not only effective but should receive marketing approval as well.

In March 1989, the FDA was persuaded that *anyone* with CMV should have access to ganciclovir. "Under pressure from officials at the National Institutes of Health and from AIDS patients and their advocates," the *New York Times* reported, "the Food and Drug Administration has decided to allow patients with the disease to receive [the] experimental drug for eye infections, even if they are not enrolled in clinical trials to test the drug."

Thirty-seven years after it was first developed, ganciclovir remains the preferred first-line treatment for cytomegalovirus.

CHAPTER 48

Parallel Trials

The ganciclovir controversy was a pivotal moment in the fight for people with AIDS. It demonstrated what the activists had been saying all along: the strict guidelines that governed experimental drug trials could not be written as one-size-fits-all policies because they risked excluding so many of the people the drugs were designed to help. Access to clinical trials was too limited. The activists wanted to make the experimental HIV/AIDS drugs available to people outside the clinical trials, arguing that race, class, gender, income, age, and health status should not be barriers to experimental treatments for any person who needed care. According to ACT UP member Mark Harrington, "People of color, women, poor people, rural people, IV-drug users, [the incarcerated], hemophiliacs, and children with HIV were routinely excluded." In the summer of 1989, activists Peter Staley, Jim Eigo, and Mark Harrington met with Dr. Fauci at his office to propose a solution to the problem. It was called parallel trials. The program created large, separate "trials" that ran parallel to the conventional clinical trials. With a simple phone call to a toll-free number, a physician from anywhere in the country could enroll their patient. In exchange for access to the experimental drugs, parallel trial participants agreed to share basic data about the drugs' effectiveness with the FDA. Fauci and the activists hammered out the details and, a few days later, Fauci announced his support of the program in the *New York Times*. The FDA followed Fauci's lead, implementing the parallel trial program "on a case-by-case basis" at the agency. Thousands of people across the US gained access to experimental drugs as a result of ACT UP's parallel trials program.

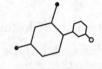

CHAPTER 49

"A Seat at the Table"

Sixth International AIDS Conference
San Francisco, California
June 1990

Peter Staley prepared to take the stage at San Francisco's Moscone Center for the opening ceremony of the Sixth International Conference on AIDS. Less than a month earlier, the twenty-nine-year-old and his fellow ACT UP members had marched on the National Institutes of Health, where Staley's arrest had been interrupted by Dr. Anthony Fauci. Since the organization's founding, ACT UP had repeatedly commanded the country's attention through strategic and large-scale protests. In the process, they had made an ally of Dr. Fauci, a man they had repeatedly and publicly called their sworn enemy.

ACT UP had made real and lasting change by successfully redefining how clinical trials were carried out in the US and kept lifesaving drugs, like ganciclovir, on the market. Since the birth of ACT UP, the NIH budget for HIV/AIDS research had tripled. Despite their hard-won victories, however, data from a CDC *Morbidity and Mortality Weekly Report* would show that by 1990, "HIV infection was the second leading cause of death among men aged 25–44 years. Among women in the same age group, it was the sixth leading cause of death." At least 160,000 Americans had perished from AIDS-related illness—twice as many as the number of Americans killed in the Vietnam War. ACT UP kept fighting back, kept fighting AIDS, because there was still no treatment or cure for the terminal disease. The needs of people with AIDS were urgent. "We didn't have time to play the long game," Peter Staley wrote.

Outside the Moscone Center, ACT UP activists were protesting a discriminatory travel ban. In effect since 1987, it barred anyone who was HIV-positive from entering the United States unless they first obtained a special waiver. If the suitcase of a foreign traveler without a waiver was found to contain AZT during a routine luggage search, that traveler could be denied entry into the US. ACT UP argued that the ban violated the civil rights of people with HIV/AIDS and reinforced the stigma against them.

Activists continued to demand more diversity in clinical trials and were willing to work with government agencies, but insisted they needed to be included in the decision-making process. Who better to help design a drug trial than the people

Discriminatory Travel Ban Against People with HIV/AIDS

The discriminatory travel ban against people with HIV/AIDS remained in place for twenty-two years. It was finally lifted by President Barack Obama in 2010.

whose lives it was meant to save? Activists insisted people with AIDS should be involved in the planning of trials from the early stages. They wanted to guarantee that trials fairly represented the population they were supposed to benefit.

With these issues in mind, Peter Staley prepared to deliver one of the most important speeches of his life. His remarks were intended to incite further action on behalf of people with AIDS. But from where he stood near the stage at San Francisco's Moscone Center, in front of the large crowd of AIDS researchers and scientists, it appeared that the city of San Francisco expected him to incite violence. "There were lines of them," Staley wrote, "in formation . . . almost two hundred police officers . . . in full riot gear."

Staley began his speech with a moment of solidarity, inviting his fellow AIDS activists to approach the stage. As they walked forward, the crowd erupted in applause. It was an encouraging sign for what Staley planned to do next: use his speech to stage a peaceful protest against President George H. W. Bush.

Bush was conspicuously absent from the conference. Rather than participate in the most important international meeting on HIV/AIDS, the president was attending a fundraiser for Senator Jesse Helms. The North Carolina lawmaker was reviled by the queer community. He introduced the Helms AIDS Amendments—standard amendments to larger bills before the Senate. The legislation forbid the use of federal funds for educational material about HIV/AIDS believed to "promote, encourage, and condone homosexual activities." The law came at a time when all people desperately needed science-based information about how to protect themselves from the virus. It had also been Helms who, in 1987, had proposed the travel ban against people with HIV that eventually became the law of the land in the US.

Bush's absence was noteworthy, but hardly surprising. His actions (and inactions) as president echoed those of his predecessor, Ronald Reagan, under whom Bush had served for eight years as vice president. He, too, was willfully neglecting one of the greatest humanitarian crises of the twentieth century, allowing more than a year to pass before publicly mentioning the AIDS epidemic that was continuing to spiral out of control on his watch. The activists were demanding that Bush do more to help people with AIDS, instead of supporting homophobic policies like the travel ban, and other homophobic politicians like Jesse Helms.

"I'd like to ask you to join us in vocalizing our collective anger," Peter Staley said to the crowd. "Join us in a chant against the man who . . . has decided to show his commitment to fighting AIDS by refusing to be here today." Then Staley began to chant. "THREE HUNDRED THOUSAND DEAD FROM AIDS! WHERE IS GEORGE?" To his delight, the audience of thousands took the cue. Rising to their feet, they joined Staley in an enthusiastic protest against George H. W. Bush's unforgivable choice to skip the conference in favor of playing politics with Helms. When the chant ended, Staley told the audience, "You can all now consider yourselves members of ACT UP."

Staley's words had ignited a spirit of solidarity that had calmed the anxious crowd. "We hadn't burned the place down," he recalled years later. "We had won them over."

Staley spoke to the audience about his personal experience with HIV. "I have always been painfully aware that in order for me to beat this virus and live, I will need a great deal of help from all of you as well as from my government. Cooperation between all of us is the fastest way to a cure . . . can we all, before it's too late, begin to understand each other? Will we realize that we share similar motivations? Can we try . . . to bridge the widening gap between us?" The crowd responded to Staley's plea with thunderous applause.

At the close of the conference a few days later, Dr. Fauci took the stage. He spoke about the state of HIV/AIDS research worldwide, then addressed the ongoing conflict between AIDS activists and the scientists who were trying to help them.

"Scientists . . . are confronted by the accusation . . . that they are not doing enough and they are moving too slowly [in response to the AIDS crisis]. The most vocal, provocative

George H. W. Bush and HIV/AIDS Legislation

Between July and August 1990, President George H. W. Bush signed two pieces of legislation that addressed the AIDS crisis. Under the Americans with Disabilities Act, discrimination against people living with HIV/AIDS was forbidden, "including employment, transportation, public accommodations, communications and access to state and local government programs and services."

The Ryan White CARE Act was named for the teenager who contracted HIV in 1984 from a blood transfusion. When the thirteen-year-old was denied entry to school after his diagnosis, he turned to activism, becoming an outspoken advocate for people with AIDS. White died in 1990, but the law that bears his name strives to improve the quality and availability of care and treatment for low-income people living with HIV. While President Bush signed these two crucial pieces of legislation, they did not originate in his office. Both laws were the result of unrelenting pressure from HIV/AIDS activists and the US Congress.

and articulate groups among these are the AIDS activists . . . They do have something important to say and they can contribute constructively to our mission. When it comes to clinical trials, some of them are better informed than many scientists can possibly imagine. Yet they are sometimes incorrect. However, we must not disregard everything that they say just because some of the things they say are incorrect . . . mistakes have been made by both sides.

"Activists are mistaken when they assume or at least publicly state that scientists do not care about them. Most scientists care deeply, and are employing all of their energies and talents to accomplish the same goals as the activists . . . To tell scientists that they are not doing enough . . . is devastating to a physician-scientist who has devoted years to AIDS research, particularly when they themselves see so many of their own patients suffering and dying . . . Scientists are experiencing repressed grief themselves. Grief and frustration that they do not have the answers for the very people whom they've been trying to help.

"On the other hand, scientists cannot and should not dismiss activists merely on the basis of the fact that they are not trained scientists . . . Activists bring a very special insight into the disease . . . they can actually be helpful in the way that we design our scientific approaches. We must join together, for together we were a formidable force with a common goal."

At the conference, ACT UP members met with Fauci. He told them that another shared goal had been reached. The activists would finally be allowed to join the executive committee of the AIDS Clinical Trials Group (ACTG), the world's largest network of HIV clinical trials. At last, people with HIV/AIDS would have a say in how trials were conducted. "We had finally won our seat at the table," Peter Staley said.

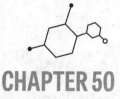

CHAPTER 50

"The Worst Years"

Despite the tremendous gains made by ACT UP on behalf of people with AIDS, the next five years were the most devastating of the American AIDS epidemic. In 1991, the World Health Organization (WHO) estimated that 10 million people worldwide were infected with HIV. The following year, AIDS was the leading cause of death in the US for men between the ages of 25 and 44. By 1994, it would become the leading cause of death for all Americans in that age group. ACT UP member David Barr said, "It was a really terrifying time."

The frontline treatment against AIDS, the drug AZT, was failing. When HIV hijacked a healthy cell, it relied on three enzymes in order to reproduce itself: protease, integrase, and reverse transcriptase. AZT worked by interrupting the production of the reverse transcriptase enzyme, which slowed the rate at which cells could produces more virus. However, as the years passed, the virus changed, or mutated, and AZT was no longer as effective. Since the mid-1980s, pharmaceutical companies had been working on new drugs to target the other enzymes without conclusive results. Then, in 1995, "we got lucky," Barr said.

That year, the FDA approved a study of saquinavir, the first drug in a new class of medications called protease inhibitors. Instead of attacking the reverse transcriptase enzyme like AZT, they attacked a different enzyme—the protease.

In the replication of HIV, the protease enzyme chops large proteins into smaller pieces. Those smaller bits of protein assemble and form the mature virus—one that is capable of infecting other cells. Like an offensive lineman protecting a vulnerable quarterback, protease inhibitors block the action of the protease enzyme, decreasing the amount of virus that is produced.

Six months after the study began, the FDA approved saquinavir and the first protease inhibitor became available to treat HIV/AIDS. More protease inhibitors followed. Doctors began prescribing the new protease inhibitors in combination with existing drugs like AZT. Together, the drugs attacked the production of the HIV at multiple stages of its development, making it harder for the virus to replicate itself. It was the birth of combination therapy, or antiretroviral therapy (ART), and it transformed the fight against HIV/AIDS.

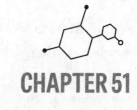

CHAPTER 51

The Lazarus Effect

People with AIDS stopped dying. Hospital beds emptied. "We were calling it the Lazarus effect," Dr. Fauci said. "People who were in hospices and people who were getting ready to die were all of a sudden starting to feel well again." He called it "one of the greatest triumphs in clinical medicine."

Peter Staley began combination therapy in 1996. "One by one, all of us became undetectable within one to three months," he wrote. Staley learned the virus was undetectable in his body on November 15, 1996—the eleventh anniversary of his diagnosis.

Thousands of people in the early days of the AIDS crisis in America didn't live long enough to benefit from combination therapy. One of them was Vito Russo. Two years before he died of AIDS in 1990, he spoke again at an ACT UP demonstration in Albany, New York. His speech encapsulated the reasons why he and his fellow activists continued to fight for the rights of people with HIV/AIDS. "When future generations ask what we did in the war, we're going to have to be able to tell them that we were out here fighting, and we have to leave a legacy to the generations of people who will come after us . . . Remember that someday the AIDS crisis is going to be over . . . And when that day . . . has come and gone, there are going to be people alive on this earth, gay people and straight people, and Black people and white people, men and women who are going to hear the story that once, a long time ago, there was a terrible disease, and that a brave group of people stood up and fought, and in some cases died, so that others might live and be free."

If the United States government had moved faster when HIV/AIDS first emerged, responding with empathy and action instead of prejudice and callousness, more lives could have been saved. The AIDS crisis in America is a model for how ordinary people can create change. It is also a reminder of what can be lost when discrimination and fear are allowed to shape the response to an outbreak.

Today, HIV/AIDS remains a serious diagnosis, but is no longer an automatic death sentence. For people who have access to, and can afford, treatment, there is hope for survival. Scientists continue to make progress in AIDS research. In 2007, an integrase inhibitor (a drug that targets another of the three enzymes that cells use to produce HIV) was developed, and in 2012 a new preventative treatment, PrEP (pre-exposure prophylaxis), became available. When used as directed, it is 99 percent effective in preventing HIV infection. As of this writing, five HIV-positive people who underwent stem cell transplants as treatment for cancer have experienced remission of their HIV. But the procedure is considered too expensive and too dangerous for any person with HIV who does not also have a life-threatening cancer diagnosis. In the meantime, scientists continue working to develop a vaccine.

HIV Today

In the US, there are 38,000 new HIV infections per year. At the end of 2021, 1.2 million people in the US were living with HIV.

These scientific achievements were driven by the demands of AIDS activists. ACT UP channeled their rage into influential acts of civil disobedience that forced the government and scientific community to pay attention to the human side of the equation. Like disease detectives, they learned everything they could about the virus in an effort to halt its spread, and helped educate the public about HIV in the hope of saving lives. The activists didn't ask for a seat at the table, they demanded it, and their unwavering resolve set the ethical standard for science during the AIDS crisis.

For Dr. Anthony Fauci, who would become one of the most frequently cited living scientific researchers, managing the government's response to the AIDS crisis changed the way he approached medicine. "I went from a listener to a colleague, to an advocate, to an activist because [the AIDS activists] were absolutely completely correct," he said. "[They have] written the book on community involvement in how the scientific and regulatory community interacts with those people that are involved."

As the fight against HIV/AIDS entered a new era, Dr. Fauci kept an eye toward the future. The world still desperately needed a vaccine against HIV. In a meeting with President Bill Clinton and Vice President Al Gore in 1996, the president asked Fauci what kind of resources he needed to do it. Fauci seized the moment, telling the president what the country needed was a facility where scientists from a wide variety of disciplines (immunology, virology, structural biology, microbiology, and bioengineering) could collaborate on an HIV vaccine. Four years later, the Vaccine Research Center (VRC) opened its doors at the National Institutes of Health.

In 2020, the VRC, which Fauci helped establish, would become ground zero in the development of an innovative vaccine to fight another deadly pandemic: COVID-19. But for many years, the technology at the heart of what would become the VRC's pandemic-crushing vaccine was considered too experimental to work. Only a small number of scientists around the world dared to believe that they could harness the power of a mysterious molecule inside the human body, called mRNA, to create disease-fighting vaccines. A number of those scientists worked for years with little or no recognition for their discoveries, never giving up, because they knew that it was only a matter of time before the next fatal virus emerged. And when it did, they would be ready.

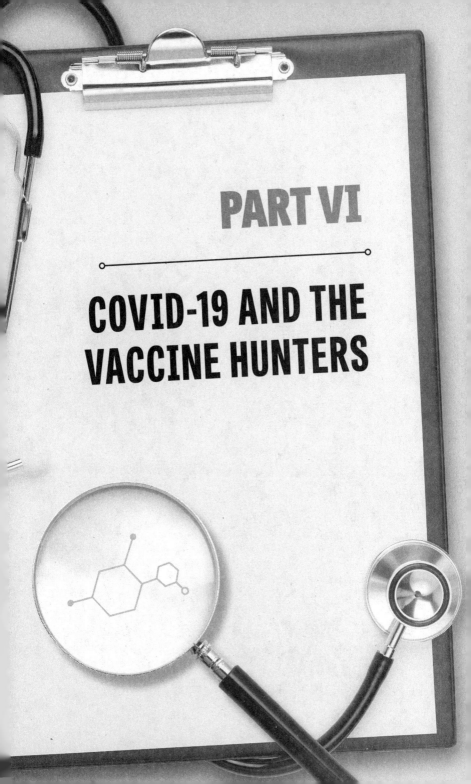

PART VI

COVID-19 AND THE VACCINE HUNTERS

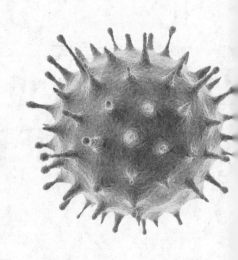

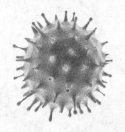

CHAPTER 52

The Teddy Bear Defection

Hungary
1985

Katalin Karikó watched nervously as her two-year-old daughter, Zsuzsanna, toddled through the airport clutching her teddy bear. Karikó and her husband, Béla Francia, were depending on their daughter to hold on to the toy. Their future was stitched inside it.

The family had a secret. They were immigrating to the United States with no immediate plans to return to their native Hungary. In order for Karikó, a biochemist, to continue what she believed was groundbreaking medical research, she had to escape her home country.

Life in communist-held Hungary had been challenging for Karikó since she was two years old. In 1957, her father, János, had spoken out against the communist government. Overnight, their middle-class life collapsed. János, a butcher, was suddenly unemployed. Money was tight, her father forced to pick up odd jobs. The family persevered through those lean years without a refrigerator or running water in their two-room house.

Because she grew up in meager circumstances, the future scientist lived a childhood free of the distractions, like television, that other kids her age enjoyed. Instead, Katalin entertained herself by playing outside, studying animals, and indulging her endless curiosity about the natural world. Katalin's grades in science reflected her love of the outdoors. By the eighth grade, she was one of Hungary's top three students in biology.

When she went off to college at Hungary's University of Szeged, Karikó had already decided to become a scientist. In 1976, she attended a lecture on a genetic molecule found inside the cells of every living thing, called mRNA—or messenger ribonucleic acid. Known as "the software of life," mRNA is crucial to the production of the proteins that your body needs to function, like antibodies, insulin, and collagen. It's called "messenger" RNA because its job inside cells is to deliver protein-making instructions to the ribosomes, the hamburger-shaped structures that manufacture the body's various proteins. After the mRNA molecule's delivery is completed, it is broken down by the cell.

Karikó learned from the lecture that it was theoretically possible for scientists to make artificial mRNA molecules that would deliver instructions for making antibodies—the proteins that fight viruses. By using artificial mRNA in this way, the body could learn to manufacture its own medicine! While it was possible to isolate mRNA from cells, the technology required to make artificial mRNA did not yet exist. But the idea struck a deep chord within the budding scientist as she realized how powerful mRNA could be in the fight against disease. In that moment, Katalin Karikó discovered her life's work.

After earning a PhD in biochemistry, Karikó began her professional career at a renowned research laboratory in Szeged. As the years passed, her obsession with artificial mRNA deepened. With the advent of PCR technology, it became possible for Karikó to create artificial mRNA. A scientist ahead of her time, she held steadfast to her belief in the molecule's potential and refused to allow any obstacle to stand in the way of discovery.

From the beginning, Karikó encountered frequent obstacles in her career. Scientists in Hungary were often short on basic laboratory supplies. Karikó patiently endured the shortages by making some of her own. When funding was cut to her laboratory, Karikó lost her job and began looking for a new position in the United States. "I never wanted to leave Hungary," she said. "But when it came time to apply for jobs, I knew I had to leave." Karikó was hired as a researcher at Temple University in Philadelphia, Pennsylvania. But first, she and her family had to escape Hungary.

The communist government banned Hungarians from leaving the country with more than $100. The small sum of money made it difficult to venture far beyond Hungary's borders, effectively trapping Hungarians behind the "Iron Curtain" of communism. To secretly raise the money for their family's journey to the US, Karikó and her husband sold their car for $1,200. Then Karikó made a small incision in her daughter's teddy bear, stuffed the cash inside, and sewed it closed.

The couple must have been relieved as they finally boarded the plane that would carry them to a new life, their daughter clutching the valuable toy bear. Behind its cheerful expression and soft round belly, the family's small nest egg was safe, snuggled close to little Zsuzsanna.

The teddy bear that Karikó and her family used to smuggle their savings out of Hungary.

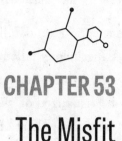

CHAPTER 53
The Misfit

By 1989, Karikó had left Temple University to accept a new research assistant professor position at the University of Pennsylvania, continuing her quest to study how to use mRNA to treat disease. Her research at Penn was not funded by the university; she was expected to raise the money herself by applying for grants. But the organizations that funded scientific research were hesitant to invest in Karikó's work. The study of mRNA was a new and unproven field. Descriptions of mRNA experiments read more like science fiction than actual science because the molecule was delicate and notoriously difficult to work with. The mRNA was destroyed after delivering its instructions to the ribosomes, making it challenging to study. Few scientists were brave enough to take it on because mRNA demanded dogged patience, meticulous attention to detail, and a stubborn refusal to quit when experiments failed. To unlock mRNA's vast potential, a scientist would have to possess another element that could not be visualized on the periodic table or explained in a research funding application—faith.

And that, Katalin Karikó possessed in abundance.

But her faith was tested almost daily by her experiments as well as her colleagues, because neither she nor her science fit in at Penn. She was treated like an outsider. But Karikó remained determined, arriving at the lab before dawn and leaving after dark because the quest for discovery fueled her—not the approval and acceptance of her coworkers.

Unfortunately, it was Karikó's passion for discovery that further complicated her position at the university. Once, during a presentation by another university scientist, Karikó rigorously questioned their work. Karikó's boss intervened, calling her "disruptive." Karikó was surprised by the reprimand because scientists are required to ask questions and challenge results in order to find the truth.

Karikó didn't require the approval of her colleagues to continue her work, but she desperately needed to win the approval of organizations that funded scientific research. When her applications were repeatedly rejected, and her research failed to yield results, Karikó's boss issued an ultimatum: she could leave Penn, or stay and be demoted to a job with less pay.

Karikó was devastated. It was 1995. She had been working as hard as she could at the school for six years. Now the university was trying to kick her out. "I thought of going somewhere else, or doing something else," she said. "I also thought maybe I'm not good enough, not smart enough . . . I just have to do better experiments."

To the university's surprise—and the dismay of her Ivy League colleagues—Karikó accepted the demotion. She was transferred to the neurology department, grateful that at least she still had a space to continue her experiments. Despite repeated setbacks inside and outside the laboratory, Karikó remained certain that mRNA was the future of medicine. It was only a matter of time until she could prove it, and she wasn't going to waste a second feeling sorry for herself.

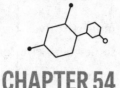

University of Pennsylvania
1998

Katalin Karikó waited patiently as the photocopier grudgingly coughed up another page of the scientific journal article she wanted to read. In the late 1990s, the scientific journals where researchers published their latest discoveries were not yet available in a digital format. Lately, Karikó kept running into the same person at the machine, another scientist who seemed to copy as many articles as she did.

Karikó glanced up from the copier and noticed he was back, hoping for a turn with the machine. She had seen Dr. Drew Weissman around the office, but they had never met. Now that they were stuck at the photocopier again, the outgoing Karikó introduced herself.

The thirty-nine-year-old immunologist was friendly but quiet, with an intense, unblinking gaze that reflected his focused mind. Unlike Karikó, he had grown up privileged in the United States as the son of an engineer and a dental hygienist. After graduation from medical school at Boston University, he had worked on HIV vaccines at the National Institutes of Health.

The title "scientist" fit Weissman as sharply as his smart white lab coat. He reveled in the quiet research that always held the promise of new discoveries. He hoped that one day his work would yield virus-killing vaccines for all kinds of disease and told Karikó that he was working on a vaccine against HIV.

Karikó, always eager to discuss possible applications of her favorite subject, synthetic mRNA, offered to help. "I am an RNA scientist," she said. "I can make anything with mRNA." If his experiments could benefit from artificial mRNA, she said with characteristic generosity, all he had to do was ask.

Weissman was intrigued by the offer. He had considered experimenting with mRNA in vaccines, and his new friend at the photocopier was willing to help. He knew mRNA was extremely difficult to work with, and yet the very challenges that chased most scientists away from mRNA seemed to draw Karikó to it. Weissman wasn't quite as excited about mRNA as Karikó. But unlike most of her critics, he told her that he was willing to give it a try. He was also willing to finance their experiments with money from his lab's budget since Karikó had not received any funding. In each other, the two scientists found a force as powerful as discovery—partnership.

Dr. Katalin Karikó and Dr. Drew Weissman in the lab at the University of Pennsylvania

They began studying ways to make Karikó's synthetic mRNA safe to use inside the body. Whenever mice were injected with it, their immune systems recognized the molecule as a foreign invader. The mRNA was attacked and destroyed before it could reach the ribosomes and deliver its protein-making instructions. The immune system's attack on the artificial mRNA triggered catastrophic inflammation in the mice's bodies. "Their fur got ruffled, they hunched up, they stopped eating; they stopped running. Nobody knew why," Dr. Weissman said. Some of the mice died. If there was going to be any hope of someday using Karikó's artificial mRNA in vaccines for people, she and Weissman had to figure out how to sneak it past the human body's natural defenses.

For nearly ten years they worked diligently in Weissman's lab, trying to solve the problem. "We were both completely open-minded," he said. "Any data that we didn't understand, and there was a lot of it, we sat down, we kept doing experiments. We kept getting results. We kept getting excited by the results."

One day, while Karikó was indulging in her hobby of reading old scientific journals, she discovered an article suggesting that one of her building blocks of synthetic mRNA, uridine, could be causing the mice's immune systems to overreact. She and Weissman wondered: What would happen if they replaced uridine with a different building block? Karikó made a new batch of the synthetic mRNA, swapping uridine for pseudouridine. When the mice received their injections with the new batch of artificial mRNA, there was no dramatic immune response, no deadly inflammation in their bodies. Their immune systems had not attacked and destroyed the artificial mRNA. The pseudouridine helped Karikó's synthetic mRNA bypass the mice's natural defenses. It was the breakthrough they had been working for!

At long last, they had discovered how to safely use synthetic mRNA. "We realized at that moment that this would be very important," Weissman said, because the discovery had the power to revolutionize the treatment of diseases in vaccines and other kinds of therapy.

In 2005, the elated scientists followed up their major discovery with the publication of a scientific paper to share their findings with the world. To Karikó and Weissman's dismay, however, no one seemed to care. "Nobody invited us anywhere to talk about it, nothing," Karikó recalled. It would take the outbreak of a mysterious virus in Wuhan, China, in early 2020 to make the wider scientific community, and the world, herald their achievement: a discovery that one day helped save millions of lives.

CHAPTER 55
Going Viral

Shanghai, China
Saturday, January 11, 2020

Virologist Dr. Yong-Zhen Zhang was exhausted when he boarded the airplane bound for Beijing. The mysterious outbreak in Wuhan was getting worse. It was Zhang's job to advise Chinese health officials about what he had discovered in fluid samples taken from the lungs of severely ill patients who had recently arrived at Wuhan Central Hospital in the Hubei province of China. They suffered from severe respiratory symptoms, but doctors were unable to determine the cause. Zhang, an internationally respected scientist who had once worked at China's version of the CDC, now worked at a public science facility near Shanghai. Eight days earlier, inside a BSL-3 lab, he had analyzed the patients' lung samples to identify the pathogen. Working around the clock for almost forty-eight hours, Zhang identified the genome sequence of the virus contained in the samples. The sequence was like an encoded message that could only be interpreted by an infectious disease expert. Zhang read the message loud and clear: coronavirus.

Coronaviruses were first discovered in the 1960s. This large family of zoonotic viruses can infect both animals and people. They're named for the spike proteins covering their surface that give them the appearance of a corona, or crown. Some coronaviruses cause intestinal illness. Others cause upper respiratory infections, like the common cold. In 2003, scientists learned that not all coronaviruses are created equal. In February of that year, a new coronavirus, SARS-CoV, was discovered in Asia. It caused the respiratory disease severe acute respiratory syndrome (SARS). Symptoms began anywhere from two to ten days after infection and included fever, chills, body aches, coughing, and shortness of breath. The virus spread around the world, infecting 8,098 people and killing 774 in more than twenty-four countries. It was the first pandemic of the twenty-first century.

In the United States, eight people who had recently traveled to countries where the virus was circulating came down with SARS, but there were no fatalities. Testing efforts, the regulation of travel, and quarantine helped end the SARS pandemic in 2004. A later investigation suggested that the virus's animal host was the masked palm civet—a raccoon-like, mostly nocturnal animal native to the Indian subcontinent and Southeast Asia.

When Zhang discovered that the virus spreading in China was a *new* coronavirus, he feared it would explode into a pandemic, like SARS. China's communist government took steps to stop the spread of the new virus—and the spread of any information about it. They closed the Huanan Seafood Wholesale Market in Wuhan, where the first cases were reported. Doctors who posted information about the mysterious illness online were arrested. Zhang was forbidden by the Chinese government to publish his findings about the virus.

Dr. Yong-Zhen Zhang

As passengers continued to board the plane to Beijing, Zhang's cell phone rang. It was his friend and scientific collaborator Dr. Edward Holmes, an evolutionary biologist and virologist at the University of Sydney in Australia. Zhang had confided in Holmes about his discovery without disclosing the virus's complete genome sequence, which was forbidden by the Chinese government. Zhang listened as Holmes pleaded with him to publicize the virus's genetic sequence. The world needed to know about the virus spreading in China, Holmes said, and offered to release the information on Zhang's behalf. So, at great personal and professional risk, Zhang agreed to give Holmes the virus's full sequence, and permission to share it.

After their call ended, Holmes received an email from Zhang containing the sequence. He logged into his Twitter social media account and composed a message:

All, an initial genome sequence of the coronavirus associated with the Wuhan outbreak is now available.

The post included a link to Virological.org, an online virology database where Holmes had uploaded Zhang's coronavirus genome sequence. At that point, anyone in the world with an internet connection could download the data. Satisfied with the content of his message, Holmes posted the tweet, and the identity of the new coronavirus went viral.

CHAPTER 56

It Was Only a Matter of Time

Vaccine Research Center
Bethesda, Maryland
January 2020

When Dr. Barney Graham got his first look at the virus's sequence, he was not surprised to learn that the cause of the outbreak in Wuhan, China, was a new coronavirus. As the deputy director of the Vaccine Research Center (VRC), part of the National Institutes of Health, he led a team of government scientists who developed vaccines for a range of infectious human diseases, including HIV, influenza, and coronaviruses.

Graham was a legend in the field of virology. He began his career as a clinical physician at Vanderbilt University in Nashville. After witnessing the ravages of AIDS on his patients in the early 1980s, he wanted to do more than treat the disease. He wanted to end it. Graham decided to become a virologist to help develop a vaccine against HIV and other pathogens, like coronaviruses.

The SARS outbreak in 2003–2004 had proved that coronaviruses could cause more severe disease than a common cold. They had pandemic potential. Graham believed that it was only a matter of time before another new coronavirus emerged to threaten global public health. He also believed that understanding the structure of coronaviruses was the key to developing effective vaccines against them.

Dr. Barney Graham

Dr. Jason McLellan thought so, too. As a structural biologist, he studied the architecture of molecules to understand their composition, how they work, and how they interact. In 2008, he was hired by another laboratory within the VRC. When he arrived, McLellan learned that the fourth-floor lab where he was assigned had more scientists than workspace. He was relocated to the second floor. That's where he met Dr. Barney Graham, who sat nearby. The older scientist told McLellan that he, too, was interested in creating vaccines that were based on a virus's structure. McLellan, who had been working on HIV, confided in Graham that he was ready to tackle something new. The scientists became friends and began collaborating on structure-based vaccines.

After McLellan left the VRC to open his own lab at Dartmouth College in 2013, the researchers continued their partnership. By this time, another new coronavirus had emerged. The Middle East respiratory syndrome coronavirus (MERS-CoV) caused a severe and contagious respiratory disease. In September of 2012, health officials in Saudi Arabia first reported cases of MERS. The symptoms included fever, shortness of breath, and cough. The new virus was deadlier than its predecessor, SARS, killing one-third of those it infected.

Like all coronaviruses, the surface of the MERS virus is covered with a crown of protein spikes. The virus uses these spike proteins to penetrate healthy cells, where they hack its normal processes, forcing it to crank out copies of the coronavirus. The MERS outbreak reinforced Graham's belief that coronaviruses were not going away. In fact, outbreaks of lethal new coronaviruses were occurring more frequently.

MERS

Since its discovery in 2012, there have been 2,600 laboratory-confirmed cases and 935 deaths from MERS, all linked to countries in and around the Arabian Peninsula. Studies suggest the virus's animal host is infected dromedary camels. As of this writing, there is no known cure for MERS or SARS.

Building on earlier discoveries from their partnership, Graham and McLellan worked together on MERS. Like other viruses they had studied, the new MERS coronavirus was a shapeshifter. The protein spikes on its surface were highly unstable. Before a spike could penetrate a cell, they knew, it first had to change its shape. If they were going to succeed in designing an effective vaccine against MERS, they needed to understand the shape-shifting abilities of its spike proteins.

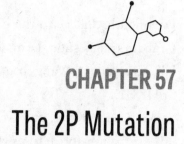

CHAPTER 57
The 2P Mutation

Graham and McLellan had been working on MERS for almost three years when a scientist at the VRC became sick with a respiratory virus. He had recently traveled to Saudi Arabia, where MERS circulated, raising fears that he had contracted the life-threatening virus. Fortunately, he recovered, and tests revealed that the scientist had not been infected with the MERS coronavirus after all. He had contracted a much milder coronavirus, known as HKU1. Their colleague's health scare gave Graham an idea. McLellan could conduct an in-depth structural study of a relatively mild (and safer) coronavirus, like HKU1, to search for clues about how to develop a vaccine against SARS, MERS, and future killer coronaviruses.

By this time, McLellan had moved his laboratory from

Dartmouth College to the University of Texas at Austin. At Graham's suggestion, he and another young researcher in his lab, Nianshuang Wang, began conducting the detailed study of HKU1.

McLellan, Wang, and Graham knew that a protein spike appears bent before it fuses with a healthy cell. But to successfully enter a cell, the spike must first lengthen and straighten. The researchers needed to find a way to lock the virus's spike protein in its pre-fusion, bent shape so the immune system could learn how to recognize coronaviruses before they could ever have a chance to multiply themselves inside a cell.

In 2014, using their knowledge of the HKU1 virus, Wang attempted to design a MERS spike protein that was almost identical to the original—but with one big difference, or mutation. He replaced two of its amino acids with a sturdier one, called proline. When they tested it in mice, the proline acted like an adhesive, holding the spike in its bent pre-fusion shape, preventing the virus from penetrating—and infecting—cells.

Wang and McLellan called it the "2P Mutation," and it was a giant leap forward in the science of vaccinology. They cowrote a scientific paper with Barney Graham describing the discovery—but despite their impressive work, it took three years for the scientists to find a scientific journal that would publish it. Coronaviruses continued to be dismissed by the scientific establishment because of their association with the common cold.

Now, three years later, the newest coronavirus had

emerged in China. This time, Barney Graham, Nianshuang Wang, Jason McLellan, and other government scientists at the VRC were ready. They had been working nonstop on coronavirus vaccine technology for years, amassing data about the viruses and how they use their spike proteins to infect cells. The team was more prepared than ever to take on the new coronavirus, and another young scientist in Graham's lab would lead the charge.

CHAPTER 58

Kizzmekia Corbett Prepares for a Pandemic

Thirty-six year-old Dr. Kizzmekia Corbett began working with Barney Graham at the Vaccine Research Center in 2014. Brilliant and bold, Corbett had known that she belonged in a scientific laboratory since she was a kid growing up in the tiny town of Hurdle Mills, North Carolina. The viral immunologist shattered the stereotypical image of a scientist, a profession historically dominated by white men.

Even as a child, Corbett was detail oriented. Myrtis Bradsher, her fourth-grade teacher at Oak Lane Elementary School, noticed that "Kizzy's" socks and shoes were perfectly matched every day. Kizzy also delighted in learning new things, and enjoyed sharing what she knew with others. A team player, she eagerly collaborated with fellow students, helping them with their assignments. Mrs. Bradsher met with

Dr. Kizzmekia Corbett

her mother and told her that Kizzy needed "a class for exceptional students."

By the time she was a tenth grader at Orange High School in Hillsborough, North Carolina, Corbett's academic talents had earned her a paid scientific summer internship through the American Chemical Society's Project SEED. The program created scientific learning opportunities for students from underrepresented groups. Through Project SEED, Corbett worked in a chemistry laboratory at the University of North Carolina at Chapel Hill. The first time she stepped inside the lab, Corbett felt like it was a second home. In that moment, she decided to become a scientist. "Even though I was young, it felt like, wow, I could really do this forever," she said.

After high school, she attended the University of

Maryland, Baltimore County, on a full scholarship, earning degrees in both biological sciences and sociology. Corbett was proud to be a "first-generation four-year graduate of college," but she didn't stop there. She returned to the laboratories at UNC-Chapel Hill to pursue a PhD in microbiology and immunology, while working for Barney Graham as a summer intern at the VRC. When they first met, Graham asked Corbett about her career aspirations. Corbett confidently replied, "I want your job." When she completed her PhD in 2014, she accepted a position working for Graham at the Vaccine Research Center.

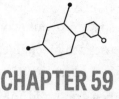

CHAPTER 59

The Vaccine Race

When the new coronavirus's sequence was first made public by Eddie Holmes and Yong-Zhen Zhang, no one in the world, including the scientists at the VRC, knew that the virus would explode into a pandemic. But Kizzmekia Corbett was ready. She was the lead scientist for the Coronavirus Vaccines & Immunopathogenesis Team at the VRC. For the past six years, she and her colleagues had been studying the MERS virus as a model, to figure out how to build better vaccines against future coronaviruses. The new virus arrived just as the technology perfected by Corbett and the VRC made it possible to design a coronavirus vaccine faster than ever before.

After downloading the virus's genome sequence, Corbett and her team scanned the sequence to choose which of its spike proteins would serve as their prototype. They would use it to bioengineer their own designer spike—one that was locked into its harmless pre-fusion bent form so it could not penetrate and infect cells. The next step was choosing the type of vaccine that would deliver their designer spike protein to the immune system.

Building a vaccine is like building a car. Think of the designer spike protein as the engine. The VRC scientists needed a vehicle to transport their spike engine into the body, where it would ignite the immune system to attack the virus. The vehicle they selected was mRNA.

When Katalin Karikó and Drew Weissman had first published their paper describing how they safely injected their synthetic mRNA into mice in 2005, almost no one had cared—no one, that is, except for Derrick Rossi. In 2005, the thirty-nine-year-old Stanford University researcher read the paper and realized the implications of the mRNA technology that Karikó and Weissman developed. He eventually used their discovery to inform his own experiments. Rossi was so encouraged by his results, and by the power of mRNA, that in 2010 he cofounded the biotechnology company Moderna. The mRNA molecule was at the heart of Moderna's mission. Even the company's name was an homage to mRNA, derived from the word "*mod*ified" and the letters *RNA*. Since 2015, the VRC had been partners with Moderna, exploring how to use mRNA technology to develop vaccines.

Traditional vaccines are manufactured in large commercial

production facilities. In some cases, the process can take as long as six months. With mRNA technology, the timeline is shorter because virus-fighting proteins are made inside the human body. The new coronavirus mRNA vaccine would also be faster to produce because scientists did not need a sample of the virus to create it. Once they had the genetic sequence of the coronavirus's spike protein, the scientists were able to genetically engineer their own "designer" spike, locked in the bent shape that the immune system could see before the virus got into a cell. This information would then be encoded into an mRNA molecule and placed in a vaccine. When the vaccine was injected into the upper arm muscle, the mRNA molecule would teach the body how to recognize the dangerous spike protein. In the event of a future attack by the coronavirus, this would enable the immune system time to identify the coronavirus and deploy the right antibodies to attack it, before the spike protein could change shape and become capable of infecting cells. After the designer mRNA molecule completed its important job, it would be destroyed as a part of normal cell function.

By the third week of January, Graham and Corbett's team at the VRC, along with Jason McLellan's lab in Texas, had developed their designer spike protein. Moderna scientists then encoded the sequence into an mRNA molecule that would deliver the spike-making instructions to cells. The experimental vaccine was complete. They called it "mRNA-1273."

The government scientists had created an innovative experimental COVID-19 vaccine in record time. But before it could be deployed against the new coronavirus, it would have to first be proven safe and effective through clinical trials—a process that could take as long as a year.

Misinformation about mRNA

During the COVID-19 pandemic, misinformation led to misunderstanding about the mRNA vaccine. Some people erroneously claimed it could alter a person's genetic makeup or cause an infection of COVID-19. Both statements are false. The synthetic mRNA molecule cannot alter a person's DNA because it does not enter the nucleus—the area of the cell that contains DNA. And the vaccine cannot cause COVID-19 because it does not contain any live virus.

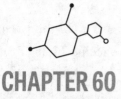

CHAPTER 60

The Gathering Storm

On January 20, what was believed to be the first case of the new coronavirus was reported in the US. Three days later, in the Chinese city of Wuhan, where the outbreak first emerged, authorities shut down all public transportation and placed 11 million people under "the largest quarantine in world history."

Nine days later, the United States of America's health and human services secretary, Alex Azar, held a press conference. "As of today," he told the assembled reporters, "CDC has reported five cases of the novel coronavirus infection here in the United States. China has now reported more than 4,500 cases. Americans should know," he continued, "that this is a potentially very serious public health threat. But at this point, Americans should not worry for their own safety."

Dr. Anthony Fauci also addressed the reporters about the vaccine under development at the VRC. "We have already started," he said. "I anticipate, with some cautious optimism, that we will be in a Phase 1 trial within the next three months . . . We are proceeding as if we will have to deploy a vaccine . . . we're looking at the worst scenario, that this becomes a bigger outbreak."

On January 31, Azar announced that the US had officially declared the new coronavirus a public health emergency. The declaration was another sign of the gathering storm, but in the minds of many Americans, the threat of the coronavirus remained a remote possibility.

By February 11, the International Committee on Taxonomy of Viruses had officially named the novel coronavirus SARS-CoV-2. The acronym stood for severe acute respiratory syndrome coronavirus 2. The disease caused by the virus was named COVID-19, an acronym for coronavirus disease and the year, 2019, in which the outbreak began. Two days later, China's National Health Commission reported that there were nearly 60,000 cases of the virus in mainland China and 1,367 deaths. More people had now died of COVID-19 than were killed in the 2003 SARS outbreak. Despite the escalation of the public health crisis at home and abroad, President Donald Trump said of the new virus: "It's going to disappear. One day—it's like a miracle—it will disappear." But the coronavirus did not disappear. By the month's end, the CDC warned that the virus could close schools and businesses, as well as other places, like theaters and sports venues.

On March 11, 2020, the World Health Organization's (WHO) director general, Dr. Tedros Adhanom Ghebreyesus, made a sobering announcement. "In the past two weeks, the number of cases of COVID-19 outside China has increased thirteen-fold, and the number of affected countries has tripled," he said. "We have therefore made the assessment that COVID-19 can be characterized as a pandemic . . . There are now more than 118,000 cases in 114 countries, and 4,291 people have lost their lives. Thousands more are fighting for their lives in hospitals."

The United States entered "lockdown," a quarantine effort by the US government designed to slow the spread of the virus. City and state school systems closed, leaving the nation's students at home. Businesses were shuttered and millions lost their jobs as the global public health crisis ballooned into an international economic crisis.

Fearful people flocked to grocery stores to stock up on food and other essentials. Soon, some of the most basic household products, like toilet paper and cleaning products, sold out entirely. The supply chains that delivered these essential items struggled to function. Supply chain workers got sick or chose not to work out of fear, resulting in global staffing shortages that interrupted the flow of goods and services around the entire world.

In what felt like an instant, life on Earth shattered. Billions of people were sheltering in place, frantically scanning newspapers and screens for answers to their questions about what was happening and how to keep safe. In the US, eventually every city, state, and town was affected by the virus, because more people were dying of COVID-19.

The only answers at the time were to stay home if possible. Wash your hands frequently. Avoid touching your face unnecessarily. Practice social distancing in public places by keeping at least six feet from others. Don't hug anyone outside your immediate household. Isolate yourself to stay alive.

Times Square in New York City was a ghost town on March 8, 2020, as US cities began to shut down in an attempt to slow the spread of COVID-19.

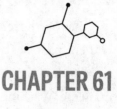

March 2020

Meanwhile, the government scientists at the VRC and their partners at Moderna were steadily gaining ground. Sixty-six days after the new virus's genome sequence was released, the mRNA-1273 vaccine was already entering the first of three phases of human clinical trials.

During Phase 1, a small group of volunteers would receive the vaccine. This first trial would measure how safe and effective the drug was, evaluate what dose level was best tolerated by the participants, and ensure that it activated a response by the immune system. Phase 2 expanded the enrollment to several hundred volunteers. In Phase 3, tens of thousands of volunteers would be vaccinated. In all three phases, participants would be monitored to test the vaccine's efficacy and safety.

One of those people was forty-three-year-old Jennifer Haller from Seattle, Washington. On March 16, 2020, at eight o'clock in the morning, she reported to the Kaiser Permanente Washington Health Research Institute, where she became the first person to receive the experimental vaccine. The vaccine was administered to forty-five participants, ranging in age from eighteen to fifty-five. Each volunteer would receive two vaccinations, twenty-eight days apart.

Haller, a mother of two, watched as reports of the pandemic grew more urgent. COVID-19 had already reached her home city of Seattle. Residents of a nearby nursing home were among the first to die as the virus swept through the facility. Area hospitals were rapidly filling with critically ill patients. As COVID-19 overtook her community, Haller wanted to do something to fight back. When she spotted a notice that volunteers were needed to test the new vaccine, she jumped at the chance. She was thrilled when her application was approved and she was selected. "I'm super proud to have a mark on history with this," she said. "I am hopeful that my participation . . . can inspire others to do something as well." Haller realized that she was in a unique position to help because she had advantages others didn't. Not only was she young, she was also healthy, with family and friends to rely on. She had a good job at a technology company that allowed her to work from home and continue to earn a living. "I wanted to do something because there's so many millions of Americans that don't have the same privilege that I've been given," she said.

The "Chinese Virus"

While patriotic Americans like Jennifer Haller used their privilege to help others during the pandemic, President Donald Trump fueled anti-Asian hate. Incidents of violence, bullying, and racist rhetoric had been on the rise around the world since the coronavirus first emerged in China. Nevertheless, the president repeatedly—and inaccurately—referred to the coronavirus in racist terms such as the "Chinese Virus" or "kung flu" when speaking to the press, or in posts to his social media accounts. The president's words, delivered from his global platform, contributed to a racist environment where hate speech—and hate crimes—could spread. By October, the organization Stop AAPI Hate had recorded 2,583 incidents of racist language against members of the Asian American and Pacific Islander communities. And in 2020, the overall number of hate crimes committed against these populations in sixteen of America's largest cities would increase by a staggering 150 percent over the previous year.

CHAPTER 62

One Molecule, Two Vaccines

The day after Moderna began the Phase 1 trial of its vaccine, Ugur Sahin, the CEO of BioNTech, another biotechnology company, announced that his company had partnered with Pfizer, a large pharmaceutical manufacturer. Together, they would also rapidly develop an experimental mRNA vaccine to fight COVID-19. Sahin, like the scientists at the VRC and Moderna, believed that mRNA could revolutionize vaccines. In 2013, he had contacted Katalin Karikó. He'd told her that he shared her belief in the future of mRNA to treat disease. He, too, wanted to use it to develop lifesaving vaccines and offered Karikó a job as a vice president at BioNTech. At the time, Karikó was still employed by the University of Pennsylvania, continuing her mRNA research. When she received the job offer, Karikó notified a university official. They laughed at her, she recalled, saying, "BioNTech doesn't even have a website." In response, Karikó accepted the new position and resigned from the university.

By 2020, BioNTech had joined forces with Pfizer, a prestigious pharmaceutical company that had been in business for over a hundred years. When the COVID-19 pandemic started, the companies were already developing a flu vaccine. In response to the global outbreak, they pivoted to developing their own mRNA vaccine against the virus. The foundation of their work was the technology perfected by Karikó and Weissman that made it safe to use mRNA inside the human body. Their discovery, which had once been largely ignored by the scientific community, became the key component of the two experimental mRNA vaccines being rapidly developed to fight the new coronavirus.

CHAPTER 63

Mask Confusion

By early April, federal health officials were urging Americans to wear a protective mask over their nose and mouth to prevent spreading the virus. In parts of the US, mask mandates went into effect. From local businesses to government offices and large corporations, employees and customers were required to "mask up." Prior to the pandemic, mask wearing wasn't common practice in the US, although people in other countries routinely wore them to guard against disease or air pollution. As the pandemic intensified, masks were embraced by many people around the world as a way to protect themselves and prevent the spread of COVID-19.

Others—including the president of the United States—argued that wearing a mask was unnecessary and ignored the recommendation altogether. "It's a recommendation, they recommend it," Donald Trump said of his own government's mask policy. "I just don't want to wear one myself." In contradicting the policy, the country's leader set a dangerous example for Americans already frustrated by the mask mandates. If the president of the United States didn't have to wear a mask, why should they?

Not everyone in the United States was fortunate to have an already healthy body when the COVID-19 pandemic struck. Among them were the elderly, and those who had preexisting health conditions—like diabetes, cancer, or other medical challenges—that put them at increased risk of death from a COVID-19 infection. Wearing a mask was a simple, effective public health strategy to help Americans protect one another from the virus.

Despite the ongoing health risks and rising death toll in the US, some state governments began pushing to reopen their economies. In early May, Dr. Anthony Fauci warned against reopening prematurely. "The consequences could be really serious," he said. "There is no doubt even under the best of circumstances when you pull back on mitigation, you will see some cases appear."

Economic hardship compounded the fear and suffering. Since mid-March 2020, 26 million people had lost their jobs because of the pandemic, and the United States passed a grim milestone: half a million confirmed cases of COVID-19 since January, and 18,600 confirmed deaths from the disease. But those numbers could not illustrate the full impact of the pandemic. A person's ability to survive could be influenced by where they lived, how much money they earned, and the color of their skin. In Chicago, Black people accounted for 68 percent of the COVID-19–related deaths but made up only 30 percent of the city's population—which meant Black people were dying of COVID-19 at a rate "nearly six times greater than that of white residents." Among the hardest hit communities were those already vulnerable due to institutional racism. Black people in low-income areas earned less money, had less access to quality healthcare, and were more likely to have jobs that required them to work outside the home. Unlike other Chicagoans with the means to work from home, some of the city's poorest people were forced to accept the increased risk in order to feed their families. Chicago's pandemic racial divide was a snapshot of what was happening in communities all across the country. The situation was also dire for historically marginalized groups of people who lived outside America's biggest cities. COVID-19 was burning out of control in the Navajo Nation. By mid-May, it would record the highest rate of infection per capita in the United States.

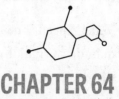

A Medical Moonshot

Friday, May 15, 2020

In mid-May, the federal government made a historic announcement. The United States was committing $18 billion to a program called Operation Warp Speed to expedite the development and delivery of vaccines for COVD-19. Operation Warp Speed promised 300 million safe and effective doses would be available by January 2021. The US had not undertaken a project on such a massive scale since NASA's Apollo program, which landed the first American on the moon in 1969. Operation Warp Speed would pay for manufacturing facilities, additional testing of vaccines, and the building of a nationwide distribution network to rapidly deliver millions of doses.

The program would also use money to speed up the vaccine manufacturing process. With funding from Operation

Warp Speed, the drug companies could begin large-scale manufacturing of vaccine doses while simultaneously testing the drugs in clinical trials. None of the steps in the human clinical trials could be rushed or skipped—that's how scientists gathered safety and efficacy data on their drugs. Should a vaccine fail to prove safe and effective in the trials, any doses already manufactured would not be used. The only thing at risk was money from the program.

Operation Warp Speed was a glimmer of hope—a strategy to help the country, and eventually the entire world, return to normal. But it would not alleviate the immediate suffering caused by the outbreak. Exhausted doctors, nurses, and other medical staff who were treating critically ill COVID-19 patients were running out of personal protective equipment (PPE). Before the pandemic, the single-use disposable items were tossed into a biohazard bin without a second thought, trusting that there was a plentiful supply. Now emergency stockpiles were depleted as manufacturers struggled to keep up with increased global demand. Many medical professionals were forced to reuse their protective face masks, placing them at increased risk of infection.

At the end of the month, the mRNA-1273 vaccine progressed to its Phase 2 clinical trial, a larger group of 600 volunteers. Half the trial participants would receive the actual vaccine, and the other half, a placebo—a harmless substance, like saline, that would have no effect in the body. The Phase 2 trial would further assess the vaccine's safety, record any adverse reactions, and measure the vaccine's ability to spark an immune response. Help could not come soon enough. By the time the Phase 2 trial began, more than 100,000 people in the United States had died of COVID-19.

Placebos

When the study's participants received their injection, they would not know if it contained the real vaccine or the placebo. However, later in the study, volunteers would be offered the chance to find out which shot they had received. At that point, those who received the placebo could choose to be vaccinated with mRNA-1273.

CHAPTER 65

"We Are Not Defenseless"

July 2020

Just as some states planned to begin the gradual reopening of businesses that had been closed for months, the United States set a frightening record, with over 75,000 new COVID-19 infections reported in a single day. More than 3 million Americans had the virus, and Dr. Fauci warned that daily cases could soar as high as 100,000. Further complicating reopening plans, the CDC released new data showing that the virus was transmitted through the air. The CDC responded by reinforcing the importance of wearing a mask while in public. "We are not defenseless against COVID-19," said CDC director Dr. Robert Redfield. "Cloth face coverings are one of the most powerful weapons we have to slow and stop the spread of the virus . . . All Americans have a responsibility to protect themselves, their families, and their communities."

By the end of the month, Moderna and Pfizer announced that their experimental mRNA vaccines had advanced to the final Phase 3 trials. Both companies would begin testing their vaccines on tens of thousands of volunteers. For Moderna and the mRNA-1273 vaccine, the celebration was short-lived. A few weeks later, their vaccine trial was in trouble. A review of its participants showed that 79 percent of those enrolled were white. Latinx, Indigenous, and Black people were not fairly represented in the study. In order for their vaccine to win approval by the Food and Drug Administration, Moderna would have to enroll more people from those diverse communities. The company responded by halting the trial to increase diversity in an effort to accurately reflect the demographics of the population.

Every person's health is determined by factors like genetics, behavior, environment, life circumstances, and lived experiences. Do they have adequate shelter? Access to clean air and water? Do they earn enough money to pay for healthy food and medical care? Someone who earns less money—or has no income—is less able to afford quality medical care, a safe place to live, or have access to clean water and enough nutritious food to eat. These conditions can disproportionately affect Black, Latinx, Hispanic, and Indigenous communities. By increasing the number of volunteers from these underrepresented groups, the trial would more accurately measure how the vaccine affected the different populations of people who received it.

It took weeks to boost enrollment, but Moderna eventually improved representation in the Phase 3 trial by adding twice as many volunteers from diverse communities to the study. The final clinical trial of their vaccine was back on track.

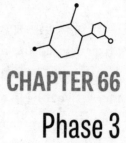

CHAPTER 66

Phase 3

As summer faded into fall, temperatures began to drop around the US, and people moved indoors. Because Americans were forced into closer quarters to escape the cold, COVID-19 infection rates soared.

In this environment, the clinical trial volunteers went about their daily lives. The pandemic put the vaccines to the ultimate test, challenging them in a real-life worst-case scenario as the deadly new coronavirus continued to spread. Only the data generated by the trial would tell scientists how well their cutting-edge vaccines were performing against COVID-19.

In early November, Pfizer became the first vaccine maker to release its Phase 3 results. The vaccine was 90 percent effective in preventing COVID-19 infection, exceeding their most optimistic projection of 70 percent. Nine days later, Pfizer revised the number from 90 to 95 percent. Not only was the world's first vaccine against the novel coronavirus an innovative mRNA vaccine, its capacity to prevent illness was astonishing.

When Pfizer senior vice president and mRNA champion Katalin Karikó learned the results of the Phase 3 trial, it was a moment of reflection and gratification for the scientist. "I didn't jump or scream," she said. "I expected that it would be very effective." As always, Karikó exuded quiet but unwavering confidence in her science, tempered with deep humility about her contributions to a lifesaving discovery. "But to help that many people," she said, "I never imagined that. It makes me very happy to know that I've played a part in this success story."

For her research partner, Drew Weissman, the news landed similarly and without fanfare. He quietly took note of the results as if they were another piece of data in an ongoing experiment. "I didn't celebrate when the Phase 3 trials came in," he said. "I had already moved on to something new . . . I'm always moving on to the next disease, the next vaccine, the next therapeutic." Weissman recalled the many years of hard work and failure that led to the vaccine. "There were a lot of down times, a lot of soul-searching, a lot of figuring out why things weren't working," he said. "But we never lost hope because we both saw the incredible potential that mRNA had."

"It was a lot of years," Karikó said. "But they weren't

boring years . . . To be a scientist is a joy."

Less than one year after the emergence of the novel coronavirus, SARS-CoV-2, scientists had successfully developed an effective vaccine to fight it. However, to beat the coronavirus, the US and the rest of the world needed multiple safe vaccines. Global COVID-19 infections continued spreading like wildfire. In the US alone, there would be 11 million cases by the middle of November, and a quarter of a million deaths. Expectations for Moderna's Phase 3 trial were high. Would it prove as effective as Pfizer's vaccine?

CHAPTER 67

A New Beginning

Seven days later, at six o'clock in the morning, Barney Graham sat down in front of the computer in his home office to place a video call to Kizzmekia Corbett. When Corbett answered, Graham told her that he had the results of Moderna's Phase 3 trial of mRNA-1273. "Well?" Corbett pressed, "What did they say?"

"There were ninety-five cases total," Graham replied. "Ninety were in the placebo group. Five were in the [vaccine group]." Corbett took a breath, her eyes wide as it dawned on her that the vaccine she had helped to create was successful beyond their wildest dreams. Graham didn't stop there. Not only was the vaccine 94.1 percent effective in preventing a case of COVID-19, he told her, the five people who had gotten sick suffered only a mild illness, "which is even better news," Graham said. Less than a year had passed since they began their race to create a vaccine. Already, it was protecting people from COVID-19 and saving lives.

"I don't even know what to say," Corbett replied, but the joyful smiles on both their faces said everything. Theirs was a story of faith and science. How a group of dedicated government researchers who were devoted to understanding a family of viruses that few others cared about proved that a virus's structure can hold the key to stopping it. And it was the story of a determined young woman from a small town in North Carolina who helped lead the team that developed a vaccine against the worst pandemic in a hundred years.

For the second time in a week, the once mystifying but infinitely powerful mRNA molecule had proven what a handful of visionary scientists had believed for decades: it had the power to save millions of lives. Moderna and Pfizer each applied for and received an Emergency Use Authorization (EUA) from the US Food and Drug Administration, so the vaccines could be immediately deployed. Operation Warp Speed lunged into gear, distributing the lifesaving shots across the country.

Operation Warp Speed Fails to Deliver on Its Distribution Promise

Operation Warp Speed set a goal of administering 20 million doses of the COVID-19 vaccine within the year. By January 1, 2021, only 3 million first doses had been administered.

CHAPTER 68

The First Shot

On Monday, December 14, 2020, just over a year after the novel coronavirus first emerged, one of Pfizer's rapidly deployed vials of vaccine was used to load a syringe at the Long Island Jewish Medical Center in New York. Nurse Sandra Lindsay rolled up her sleeve and became the first American outside of a clinical trial to be vaccinated against COVID-19.

Since that moment, other types of COVID-19 vaccines have become available and billions of people around the world have been vaccinated. These vaccines changed the course of the pandemic, making it possible to return to work, reopen schools and businesses, and hug loved ones without the fear of getting sick.

Dr. Anthony Fauci, director of the NIH, watches as President Joe Biden greets Dr. Kizzmekia Corbett at the Vaccine Research Center in 2022.

However, the COVID-19 pandemic is not over. Globally, 2.3 billion people are unvaccinated as of this writing. The lowest vaccination rates occur in countries of Africa, where vulnerable populations may lack the resources to build and fund vaccination programs. Meanwhile, wealthy countries report higher vaccination rates because their citizens have more access to the lifesaving shots. As the virus spreads, making billions more copies of itself, the structure of those copies varies slightly from the original. These slight changes, or mutations, can make the virus more contagious and cause more severe disease. Some mutations have enabled the virus to evade the immune systems of vaccinated people and make them sick. Viruses with these new types of mutations are called variants.

COVID-19 Variants and the Vaccines

According to the World Health Organization, "In general, the COVID-19 vaccines are very effective at preventing serious illness, hospitalization and death from all current virus variants. They are less effective at protecting you against infection and mild disease than they were for earlier virus variants; but if you do get ill after being vaccinated, your symptoms are more likely to be mild."

Some virologists believe that COVID-19 is on track to become an endemic disease, a persistent and possibly seasonal illness, like the flu. In the meantime, scientists around the world continue to study how well the COVID-19 vaccines guard against infection. Booster shots have been recommended in order to maintain robust protection against variants.

Other mysteries about the new coronavirus, like its source, continue to challenge scientists. Some believe that SARS-CoV-2 was the result of a spillover event—an infection that was transmitted from an animal to humans. Research into the virus's precise origins is ongoing.

What we do know is that many of the scientists who helped develop the COVID-19 vaccines, like countless other virus hunters and disease detectives throughout history, worked in relative obscurity—some of them for decades. It is thanks to scientists like Katalin Karikó, Drew Weissman, Barney Graham, Kizzmekia Corbett, Jason McLellan, Nianshuang Wang, and others that safe and effective vaccines against COVID-19 were developed and manufactured in record time. In October 2023, Dr. Katalin Karikó and Dr. Drew Weissman were jointly awarded the Nobel Prize in Physiology or Medicine for their work with mRNA that led to the development of vaccines against COVID-19.

Imagine for a moment how different the world might be without those in the field of public health who believe that the actions of just one person could make a difference. What if John Snow had never gone in search of the source of the cholera outbreak on Broad Street? What if the ACT UP activists and Dr. Anthony Fauci had stopped looking for ways to make clinical trials more inclusive for people with HIV/AIDS? What if Katalin Karikó, Drew Weissman, Barney Graham, and Kizzmekia Corbett had given up on mRNA and the study of coronaviruses? Would smallpox have been eradicated without people like Bill Foege, Mary Guinan, Cornelia Davis, and the hundreds of thousands of Indigenous public health workers worldwide who united to destroy the dreaded disease once and for all?

Inspired by these revolutionary changemakers, you can make a difference, too. Start by minimizing the risk of an outbreak within your community. Stay current on vaccines, wash your hands, and cover your mouth when you cough or sneeze. If you are sick and able to stay home, don't go to school or work, where you might make others sick, too. These may seem like insignificant actions, but they can have a huge impact on public health, especially during cold and flu season. Most of the time, preventing the spread of infectious disease really is that simple.

Outbreaks and pandemics are scary. There's no getting around it. But there are dedicated public health defenders who are ready to help in these times of crisis. When they combine their willingness to serve communities with common sense, scientific facts, and the unwavering belief that even just one person can make a difference, not only do they save lives, they change the world.

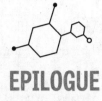

An Outbreak of Hope

In the summer of 2022, the next generation of public health defenders gathered at the CDC's David J. Sencer CDC Museum in Atlanta, Georgia, to attend Disease Detective Camp. The weeklong program is for young adults who aspire to careers in public health—like NASA Space Camp for future disease detectives.

The CDC was closed to visitors during the first two years of the COVID-19 pandemic. By 2022, vaccines and other public health measures, like COVID-19 testing and masks, made it possible to reopen the agency's museum. Disease Detective Camp was back in session.

The group of teens at the camp were different from those who attended in previous years. Their lives had been forever changed by the new coronavirus. All of them knew firsthand what it was like to live through a once-in-a-century pandemic that led to a global lockdown. Their schools had closed, forcing them to attend classes online. They missed dances, parties, proms, and sports events or, more tragically, lost friends, acquaintances, or loved ones to COVID-19.

The campers, who came from all around the world, had their own reasons for attending. One hoped to become a microbiologist and work with deadly viruses in a level 4 hot lab. Another wanted to study diseases as a geneticist. A teen from Switzerland traveled all the way to Atlanta because she wanted to become a doctor. Together, the group tackled tough public health challenges in fast-paced mock-outbreak scenarios.

Working as a team of disease detectives in the first outbreak simulation, they tracked down the source of food poisoning at a taco bar. In another, they halted an outbreak of meningitis on a college campus. The junior disease detectives also

A CDC Disease Detective Camp attendee charts her team's data from a mock-outbreak investigation.

explored public health history in the museum's many exhibits: John Snow and the Broad Street pump; the eradication of smallpox; 1918 influenza; the HIV/AIDS crisis; and the Korean hantavirus outbreak that led to the founding of the Epidemic Intelligence Service at the CDC. They learned that many past graduates of the CDC's Disease Detective Camp went on to have careers in public health, and that some of them now work for the agency.

As the diverse group became friends, they learned that they shared common goals. All of them wanted to make the world safer by helping people who were sick and searching for ways to prevent another pandemic like COVID-19. These future disease detectives are cause for hope in the ongoing fight against infectious disease, because no matter what happens, more help is on the way.

Future public health defenders: the 2022 class of CDC Disease Detective Camp graduates

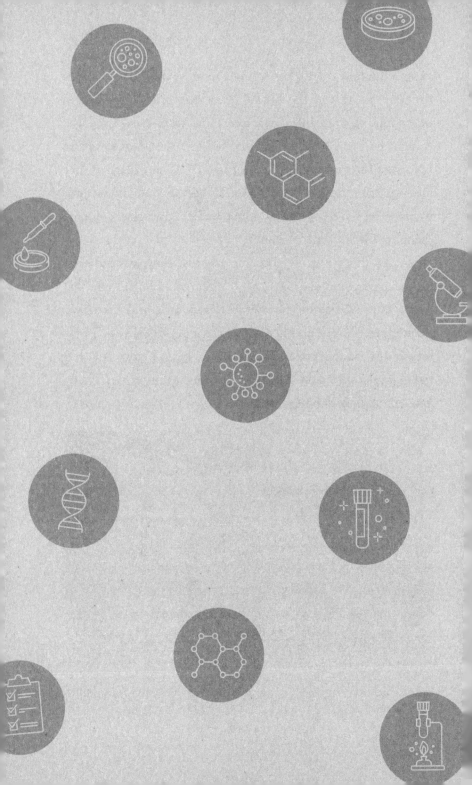

Acknowledgments

When the COVID-19 global lockdown began in March 2020, I, like billions of other people, was scared and confused. To combat feelings of helplessness, I immersed myself in primary source material about pandemics throughout history. I read scores of books, newspaper articles, government documents, scientific journals, and blogs by public health workers, physicians, virologists, epidemiologists, and vaccinologists, looking for any shred of hope. The more I learned, the better I understood that, thanks to public health professionals worldwide, we are never alone in the fight against infectious diseases. I was honored to correspond with and interview some of these talented public health defenders while researching and writing *Virus Hunters*.

Former Epidemic Intelligence Service officer Dr. Seema Yasmin and Dr. Eric Pevzner, chief of the Epidemiology and Laboratory Workforce Branch of the EIS at CDC, contributed their insight into the lifesaving work of the CDC disease detectives, past and present. Dr. Neil Vora recounted his time as an EIS officer, sharing the impact of smallpox on his family and offering valuable information about the ongoing threat posed by zoonotic viruses. Dr. Cornelia "Connie" Davis told me the incredible story of her time working in the smallpox eradication program in India. Dr. James Cheek, retired captain of the US Public Health Service (USPHS), detailed his former work as an EIS officer and physician with the Indian Health Service, as well as his experiences investigating the 1993 hantavirus outbreak. I'm also grateful to Dr. Cheek for fact-checking the hantavirus section of this book. Dr. Jamie Childs, former chief of the Viral and Rickettsial Zoonoses Branch at CDC, introduced me to *Peromyscus maniculatus* and answered questions about his role in the 1993 hantavirus outbreak investigation. Dr. Todd Smith, microbiologist in the CDC's Poxvirus and Rabies Branch, described what it's like to work in a level 4 biosafety laboratory and allowed me to try on a positive pressure biosafety suit (an experience I'll never forget!). Thank you to the staff of the David J. Sencer CDC Museum in Atlanta, Georgia, who hosted me at Disease Detective Camp, especially Mary Hilpertshauser and Trudi Ellerman. Thanks also to the 2022 Disease Detective Camp attendees for permitting me to observe their experiences, and for their dedication to the future of public health!

Brian Young and Peter Staley shared their insight into portions of the manuscript that were written outside of my lived experience. Brian provided feedback on the portrayal of Dinè (Navajo) culture in the book, as well as the geography of the Four Corners region. Peter Staley spoke with me in an interview about living with HIV and his activism career. Peter also reviewed and provided feedback on the chapters about HIV/AIDS. Activist Sarah Schulman answered questions about ACT UP and the ACT UP

Historical Archive (actupny.org). I am also indebted to Dr. Ralph Frerichs, professor emeritus in the department of epidemiology at UCLA's Fielding School of Public Health, who fact-checked the cholera section of *Virus Hunters*.

Dr. Anna Berge, professor of linguistics and director of the Alaska Native Language Archive at the University of Alaska Fairbanks, corresponded with me about the language of the Iñupiat People. Dr. Garret J. McDonald, visiting assistant professor of history at Kenyon College, fact-checked the book's historical elements. Dr. Iris Holmes of the Cornell Institute of Host-Microbe Interactions and Disease reviewed the book's scientific terms and processes for clarity and accuracy.

The top-notch editorial team at HarperCollins was with me every step of the way! Thank you to executive editor Kristin Rens, editorial assistant Christian Vega, production editor Caitlin Lonning, managing editor Gwen Morton, and designers Corina Lupp and Jessie Gang.

A million thank-yous to literary agent extraordinaire Joan Paquette for advice and wise counsel of all kinds. I'm deeply grateful to friends Janet Daniels and Paula Yoo, who are superb writers and sounding boards.

Last, but never least, thank you to my mom, Marty Keener Cherrix, and partner, Casey McCormick, for their boundless patience and love throughout the writing of *Virus Hunters*. I couldn't do any of this without you.

Bibliography

AJMC Staff. "A Timeline of COVID-19 Developments in 2020." *American Journal of Managed Care*, January 1, 2021. www.ajmc .com/view/a-timeline-of-covid19-developments-in-2020.

American Museum of Natural History. "Online Exhibition: Smallpox," 2022. www.amnh.org/explore/science-topics/disease-eradication/ countdown-to-zero/smallpox.

Andrejko, Kristin L., et al. "Effectiveness of Face Mask or Respirator Use in Indoor Public Settings . . ." *Morbidity and Mortality Weekly Report* 71, no. 6 (February 11, 2022): 212–16. www.cdc.gov/ mmwr/volumes/71/wr/mm7106e1.htm.

Associated Press. "Trump Touts 'Operation Warp Speed' in Vaccine Hunt." May 15, 2020. www.youtube.com/watch?v=SVfgYJwoVZg.

Aubrey, Allison. "Sandra Lindsay Got the First U.S. COVID Jab. Here's Her Secret to Motivate Others." NPR, December 13, 2021. www.npr.org/sections/health-shots/2021/12/13/1063020183 /sandra-lindsay-got-the-first-u-s-covid-jab-heres-her-secret-to -motivate-others.

Baden, Lindsey R., Hana M. El Sahly, Brandon Essink, Karen Kotloff, Sharon Frey, Rick Novak, David Diemert, et al. "Efficacy and Safety of the mRNA-1273 SARS-CoV-2 Vaccine." *New England Journal of Medicine* 384, no. 5 (February 4, 2021): 403–16. doi.org/10.1056/NEJMoa2035389.

Basler, Roy P. "Did President Lincoln Give the Smallpox to William H. Johnson?" *Huntington Library Quarterly* 35, no. 3 (May 1972): 279–84. www.jstor.org/stable/3816663.

Benk, Ryan, Noel King, and Reena Advani. "Skepticism of Science in a Pandemic Isn't New. It Helped Fuel the AIDS Crisis." NPR, May 23, 2021, sec. Health. www.npr.org/2021/05/23/996272737 /skepticism-of-science-in-a-pandemic-isnt-new-it-helped-fuel-the -aids-crisis.

Benner, Katie, et al. "U.S. Reports More than 70,000 New

Coronavirus Cases for the Second Time." *New York Times*, July 17, 2020. www.nytimes.com/2020/07/17/world/coronavirus-cases-update.html.

Bernard, Diane. "Three Decades before Coronavirus, Anthony Fauci Took Heat from AIDS Protesters." *Washington Post*, May 20, 2020. www.washingtonpost.com/history/2020/05/20/fauci-aids-nih-coronavirus/.

Biswas, Soutik. "Coronavirus: What India Can Learn from the Deadly 1918 Flu." BBC, March 18, 2020. www.bbc.com/news/world-asia-india-51904019.

Blanco, Lydia. "Prior to COVID-19, Dr. Kizzmekia S. Corbett Was Formulating Success as a Black Woman in Science." Black Enterprise. April 2, 2020. www.blackenterprise.com/prior-to-covid-19-dr-kizzmekia-corbett-was-formulating-success-as-a-black-woman-in-science/.

Blanding, Michael. "A Dose of Hope." Vanderbilt University, March 17, 2021. news.vanderbilt.edu/2021/03/17/shot-in-the-arm-groundbreaking-covid-19-vaccine-research-by-alumnus-dr-barney-graham-began-at-vanderbilt-decades-ago/.

Borowski, Susan. "The Virus That Rocked the Four Corners Reemerges." American Association for the Advancement of Science (AAAS), January 8, 2013. www.aaas.org/virus-rocked-four-corners-reemerges.

Borrell, Brendan. *The First Shots: The Epic Rivalries and Heroic Science Behind the Race to the Coronavirus Vaccine*. Boston: Mariner Books, 2022.

Brain, Jessica. "The Victorian Workhouse." Historic UK, August 8, 2019. www.historic-uk.com/HistoryUK/HistoryofBritain/Victorian-Workhouse/.

Breman, Joel. "Donald Ainslie Henderson (1928–2016)." *Nature* 538, no. 7623 (October 2016): 42. doi.org/10.1038/538042a.

Brilliant, Lawrence B. *Sometimes Brilliant: The Impossible Adventure of a Spiritual Seeker and Visionary Physician Who Helped Conquer the Worst Disease in History*. New York: HarperOne, 2016.

Bruchac, Joseph. *Navajo Long Walk: The Tragic Story of a Proud Peoples' Forced March from Their Homeland*. Washington, DC: National Geographic Society, 2002.

Buhles, William C. "Compassionate Use: A Story of Ethics and Science in the Development of a New Drug." *Perspectives in Biology and Medicine* 54, no. 3 (2011): 304–15. doi.org/10.1353/pbm.2011.0027.

Bunker, A. "*Peromyscus maniculatus*." Animal Diversity Web. (2001) Accessed December 12, 2023. animaldiversity.org/accounts /Peromyscus_maniculatus/.

Burki, Talha. "Global Shortage of Personal Protective Equipment." *Lancet Infectious Diseases* 20, no. 7 (July 2020): 785–86. doi.org/10.1016/S1473-3099(20)30501-6.

Butler, Jay, Thomas Ksiazek, and James Childs. "Of Mice and Men: Discovering a Deadly Hantavirus in the Americas." We Were There lecture series, August 15, 2018, Atlanta, GA. www.cdc.gov/os /wewerethere/hantavirus/index.html.

Byerly, Carol R. "The U.S. Military and the Influenza Pandemic of 1918–1919." *Public Health Reports* 125, Suppl 3 (2010): 82–91.

———. "The Influenza Pandemic of 1918–1919." Gilder Lehrman Institute of American History: AP US History Study Guide, n.d. ap.gilderlehrman.org/history-by-era/essays/influenza-pandemic -1918%E2%80%931919.

Cancryn, Adam. "Fauci Warns Reopening Country Too Fast Could Be 'Really Serious' for States." Politico, May 12, 2020. www.politico .com/news/2020/05/12/anthony-fauci-senate-testimony-coronavirus -251233.

CBS News Staff. "Activists Look Back at Anniversary of Historic San Francisco ACT UP Protests." CBS News, June 19, 2019. www .cbsnews.com/sanfrancisco/news/activists-30th-anniversary -historic-act-up-protests-san-francisco/.

Center for the Study of Hate & Extremism (CSUSB). "Fact Sheet: Anti-Asian Prejudice March 2020." 2020. www.csusb.edu/sites/default /files/FACT%20SHEET-%20Anti-Asian%20Hate%202020%20 3.2.21.pdf.

Centers for Disease Control and Prevention (CDC). "2022–2023 Mpox Outbreak Global Map." December 1, 2023. www.cdc.gov/poxvirus /mpox/response/2022/world-map.html.

———. "CDC Calls on Americans to Wear Masks to Prevent COVID-19 Spread." CDC Press release, July 14, 2020. archive.cdc.gov/# /details?url=https://www.cdc.gov/media/releases/2020/p0714 -americans-to-wear-masks.html.

———. "CDC Museum COVID-19 Timeline." n.d. www.cdc.gov /museum/timeline/covid19.html.

———. "CDC SARS Response Timeline." April 26, 2013. stacks.cdc .gov/view/cdc/44683.

———. "Flu Fighter: Terrence Tumpey, Ph.D." May 14, 2018.

www.cdc.gov/flu/pandemic-resources/1918-commemoration
/pandemic-flu-fighter-terrence-tumpey.htm.

———. "Frequently Asked Questions about SARS." May 3, 2005.
archive.cdc.gov/#/details?url=https://www.cdc.gov/sars/about
/faq.html.

———. "History of Smallpox." February 20, 2021. www.cdc.gov
/smallpox/history/history.html.

———. "HIV Basics." May 22, 2023. www.cdc.gov/hiv/basics
/statistics.html.

———. "How Influenza (Flu) Vaccines Are Made." November 3, 2022.
www.cdc.gov/flu/prevent/how-fluvaccine-made.htm.

———. "How Vaccines Are Developed and Approved for Use." March
30, 2023. www.cdc.gov/vaccines/basics/test-approve.html.

———. "Middle East Respiratory Syndrome (MERS)." August 2, 2019.
www.cdc.gov/coronavirus/mers/about/index.html.

———. "Mortality Attributable to HIV Infection/AIDS Among Persons
Aged 25–44 Years—United States, 1990, 1991." *Morbidity and
Mortality Weekly Report* 42, no. 25 (July 2, 1993): 481–86. www
.cdc.gov/mmwr/preview/mmwrhtml/00021017.htm.

———. "Notice of Embargo of Civets." May 3, 2005. archive.cdc.gov/#
/details?url=https://www.cdc.gov/sars/media/civet-ban.html.

———. "Outbreak of Hantavirus Infection in Yosemite National Park."
September 17, 2012. www.cdc.gov/hantavirus/outbreaks/yosemite
/index.html.

———. "Outbreak of Hantavirus Infection—Southwestern United
States, 1993." *Morbidity and Mortality Weekly Report* 42, no. 25
(July 2, 1993): 495–96, www.cdc.gov/mmwr/preview
/mmwrhtml/00021036.htm.

———. "Plague: Ecology and Transmission." July 31, 2019. www.cdc
.gov/plague/transmission/index.html.

———. "Plague: Frequently Asked Questions." November 15, 2021.
www.cdc.gov/plague/faq/index.html.

———. "Reported Cases of Hantavirus Disease." April 25, 2023. www
.cdc.gov/hantavirus/surveillance/index.html.

———. "Smallpox: Clinical Disease." December 5, 2016. www.cdc.gov
/smallpox/clinicians/clinical-disease.html.

———. "The 1918 Flu Pandemic: Why It Matters 100 Years Later."
Publics Health Matters (blog), May 14, 2018. blogs.cdc.gov
/publichealthmatters/2018/05/1918-flu/.

———. "Transmission: How Does Smallpox Spread?" June 7, 2016.

www.cdc.gov/smallpox/transmission/index.html.

———. "Understanding How COVID-19 Vaccines Work." September 22, 2023. www.cdc.gov/coronavirus/2019-ncov/vaccines/different-vaccines/how-they-work.html.

———. "Vaccine Effectiveness: How Well Do Flu Vaccines Work?" February 8, 2023. www.cdc.gov/flu/vaccines-work/vaccineeffect.htm.

———. "What Is Anthrax?" February 15, 2022. www.cdc.gov/anthrax/basics/.

Chu, Laurence, Roderick McPhee, Wenmei Huang, Hamilton Bennett, Rolando Pajon, Biliana Nestorova, and Brett Leav. "A Preliminary Report of a Randomized Controlled Phase 2 Trial of the Safety and Immunogenicity of mRNA-1273 SARS-CoV-2 Vaccine." *Vaccine* 39, no. 20 (May 2021): 2791–99. doi.org/10.1016/j.vaccine.2021.02.007.

Claeson, Mariam, and Ronald Waldman. "Cholera through History." *Britannica*, n.d. www.britannica.com/science/cholera/Cholera-through-history.

Cohen, Elizabeth, and Dana Vigue. "COVID-19 Vaccine Trials Have Been Slow to Recruit Black and Latino People—and That Could Delay a Vaccine." CNN, August 16, 2020. www.cnn.com/2020/08/16/health/covid-19-vaccine-trial-black-minority-recruitment/index.html.

Cohen, Patricia. "Jobless Numbers Are 'Eye-Watering' but Understate the Crisis." *New York Times*, April 23, 2020. www.nytimes.com/2020/04/23/business/economy/unemployment-claims-coronavirus.html.

Colangelo, Gabrielle, ed. "We Are Everywhere: Lesbians in the Archive." Yale University Library Online Exhibitions, 2022. onlineexhibits.library.yale.edu/s/we-are-everywhere/item/17463#?c=&m=&s=&cv=&xywh=-2564%2C1008%2C7263%2C2483.

Cole, Thom. "Mystery Flu Death Toll at 8." *Albuquerque Journal* (May 28, 1993): Morning edition.

Concar, David. "Protests Oust Science at AIDS Conference." *Nature* 345 (June 28, 1990): 753.

Conversations with Pathologists: Jeffery Taubenberger, November 27, 2007. conversations.pathsoc.org/index.php?option=com_content&view=article&id=92:jeffery-taubenberger-full-transcript&catid=11:jeffery-taubenberger&Itemid=199.

Corbett, Kizzmekia. "A Conversation with Dr. Kizzmekia Corbett: From Project SEED Student to Leading COVID-19 Researcher." By

Racquel Jemison. October 22, 2020. www.acs.org/content/acs/en /acs-webinars/library/project-seed.html.

———. "Kizzmekia Corbett: Scientist, Vaccine Developer, and Tar Heel." University of North Carolina Chapel Hill. May 13, 2021. www.youtube.com/watch?v=-27Rn0prMw0.

———. "Kizzmekia Corbett: 'Vaccines' (11/10/2020)." MIT Department of Biology, November 14, 2020. www.youtube.com /watch?v=xpqfdr9FPWM.

———. "Preparing for a Pandemic: Dr. Kizzmekia Corbett." The Franklin Institute. April 30, 2021. www.youtube.com /watch?v=_8h4fDVqGls.

———. "SARS-CoV-2 mRNA Vaccine Development Enabled by Prototype Pathogen Preparedness." October 15, 2020. videocast .nih.gov/watch=38864.

Corbett, Kizzmekia S., Darin K. Edwards, Sarah R. Leist, Olubukola M. Abiona, Seyhan Boyoglu-Barnum, Rebecca A. Gillespie, Sunny Himansu, et al. "SARS-CoV-2 mRNA Vaccine Design Enabled by Prototype Pathogen Preparedness." *Nature* 586, no. 7830 (August 5, 2020): 567–71. doi.org/10.1038/s41586-020-2622-0.

Cox, David. "How mRNA Went from a Scientific Backwater to a Pandemic Crusher." *Wired*, December 2, 2020. www.wired.co.uk /article/mrna-coronavirus-vaccine-pfizer-biontech.

Crosby, Alfred W. *America's Forgotten Pandemic: The Influenza of 1918*, 2nd ed. New York: Cambridge University Press, 2003.

Cross, Ryan. "The Tiny Tweak Behind COVID-19 Vaccines." *Chemical & Engineering News*, September 29, 2020. cen.acs.org /pharmaceuticals/vaccines/tiny-tweak-behind-COVID-19/98/i38.

David J. Sencer CDC Museum. "Smallpox Eradication." n.d. www.cdc. gov/museum/pdf/cdcm-pha-stem-lesson-smallpox-eradication-slides .pptx.

———. "Smallpox Eradication." May 27, 2021. www.cdc.gov/museum /online/story-of-cdc/smallpox/index.html.

———. "Smallpox Eradication." n.d. www.cdc.gov/museum/pdf/cdcm -pha-stem-lesson-smallpox-eradication-lesson.pdf.

Davies, Dave. "Long Before COVID-19, Dr. Anthony Fauci 'Changed Medicine in America Forever.'" NPR, April 16, 2020. www.npr.org /sections/health-shots/2020/04/16/834873162/long-before-covid-19 -dr-tony-fauci-changed-medicine-in-america-forever.

Davies, Pete. *Catching Cold*. London: Penguin Books, 1999.

Davis, Cornelia E. *Searching for Sitala Mata: Eradicating Smallpox in*

India, 2nd ed. Laredo, Texas: Konjit Publications, 2018.

Davis, Kenneth C. *More Deadly Than War: The Hidden History of the Spanish Flu and the First World War.* New York: Henry Holt and Company, 2018.

Defoe, Daniel, and Cynthia Wall. *A Journal of the Plague Year.* Penguin Classics. New York: Penguin Books, 2003.

Desai, Rishi. "Naming the Flu: H-Something, N-Something." Khan Academy, January 11, 2013. www.khanacademy.org/science /health-and-medicine/infectious-diseases/influenza/v/naming-the -flu-h-something-n-something.

Dhama, Kuldeep, Sharun Khan, Ruchi Tiwari, Shubhankar Sircar, Sudipta Bhat, Yashpal Singh Malik, Karam Pal Singh, Wanpen Chaicumpa, D. Katterine Bonilla-Aldana, and Alfonso J. Rodriguez-Morales. "Coronavirus Disease 2019—COVID-19." *Clinical Microbiology Reviews* 33, no. 4 (June 24, 2020): doi.org/10.1128/CMR.00028-20.

Donnelly, C. A., M. R. Malik, A. Elkholy, S. Cauchemez, and M. D. Van Kerkhove. "Worldwide Reduction in MERS Cases and Deaths Since 2016." *Emerging Infectious Diseases* 25, no. 9 (September 2019): 1758–1760. doi.org/10.3201/eid2509.190143.

Durr, Eric. "Flu Outbreak Killed 45,000 U.S. Soldiers during World War I." United States National Guard, August 30, 2018. www .nationalguard.mil/News/Article/1616713/flu-outbreak-killed -45000-us-soldiers-during-world-war-i/.

Eigo, Jim. "ACT UP Oral History Project." By Sarah Schulman. March 5, 2004. actuporalhistory.org/numerical-interviews/047-jim-eigo.

Elton, Catherine. "The Untold Story of Moderna's Race for a COVID-19 Vaccine." *Boston*, June 4, 2020. bostonmagazine.com/health /2020/06/04/moderna-coronavirus-vaccine/.

Fauci, Anthony. "A Conversation with Dr. Anthony Fauci." By Peter Staley. October 26, 2022. Harvard Kennedy School Institute of Politics. iop.harvard.edu/forum/conversation-dr-anthony-fauci.

———. "Anthony Fauci Speech at the Sixth International AIDS Conference." San Francisco, June 26, 1990. www.c-span.org /video/?c4970850/hd-16443-fauci-clip-9.

———. "Edward M. Kennedy Oral History Project." By Janet Heininger. September 10, 2007. www.emkinstitute.info/resources /anthony-s-fauci-oral-history.

———. "In Their Own Words . . . NIH Researchers Recall the Early Years of AIDS." By Dr. Victoria Harden and Dennis Rodrigues.

June 29, 1993. history.nih.gov/display/history/Dr+Anthony+S+Fauci
+Interview+03+June+29+1993.

———. "In Their Own Words . . . NIH Researchers Recall the Early
Years of AIDS." By Dr. Victoria Harden. March 7, 1989. history
.nih.gov/display/history/Dr+Anthony+S+Fauci+Interview+02+
March+7+1989.

———. "Q&A: PEPFAR Architect Anthony Fauci on the Initiative's
Transformational Impact." By Michael Igoe. June 8, 2018. www
.devex.com/news/q-a-pepfar-architect-anthony-fauci-on-the
-initiative-s-transformational-impact-92909.

———. "In Their Own Words . . . NIH Researchers Recall the Early
Years of AIDS." By Gerri Blumberg. 1986. history.nih.gov/display
/history/Dr+Anthony+S+Fauci+Interview+01+July+3+1986.

Fears, Darryl. "Kizzmekia Corbett Spent Her Life Preparing for
This Moment. Can She Create the Vaccine to End a Pandemic?"
Washington Post, May 6, 2020, sec. Climate and Environment.
www.washingtonpost.com/climate-environment/2020/05/06
/kizzmekia-corbett-vaccine-coronavirus/.

Fehervari, Zoltan. "Origin Story." *Nature*, November 28, 2018. www
.nature.com/articles/d42859-018-00008-6.

Foege, William H. *House on Fire: The Fight to Eradicate Smallpox*.
California/Milbank Books on Health and the Public vol. 21. Berkeley:
University of California Press; Milbank Memorial Fund, 2011.

Forensic Files. Season 4, episode 12, "With Every Breath." Produced by
Medstar Television. Aired December 22, 1999. www.youtube.com
/watch?v=HaYV41NbM9k.

France, David, dir. *How to Survive a Plague*. Public Square Films, 2012.

Frerichs, Ralph R. "Who First Discovered *Vibrio cholera*?" UCLA, n.d.
https://www.ph.ucla.edu/epi/snow/firstdiscoveredcholera.html.

Frist, Bill. "How a Rock Star, a Physician-Legislator, and an Evangelical
Senator Bonded to Help End the Global AIDS Pandemic: A
Backstory." *Forbes*, December 1, 2022. www.forbes.com/sites
/billfrist/2022/12/01/how-a-rock-star-a-physician-legislator-and-an
-evangelical-senator-bonded-to-help-end-the-global-aids-pandemic
-a-backstory/?sh=2f392bbf2fdd.

Gale, Catherine, and Caleb Hellerman. *Race for the Vaccine: A CNN
Film*. CNN Films, 2021.

Ganguly, Prabarna. "Retrovirus." National Human Genome Research
Institute, April 9, 2023. www.genome.gov/genetics-glossary
/Retrovirus.

Ganneri, Namrata. "These Memoirs Show Us the Role Women Had in Eradicating Smallpox from India." The Conversation, November 26, 2019. theconversation.com/these-memoirs-show-us-the-role-women-had-in-eradicating-smallpox-from-india-123897.

Garde, Damian, and Jonathan Saltzman. "The Story of mRNA: How a Once-Dismissed Idea Became a Leading Technology in the Covid Vaccine Race." StatNews.com, November 10, 2020. www.statnews.com/2020/11/10/the-story-of-mrna-how-a-once-dismissed-idea-became-a-leading-technology-in-the-covid-vaccine-race/.

Ghebreyesus, Tedros A. "Coronavirus Outbreak: WHO Declares COVID-19 a Global Pandemic." Global News. March 11, 2020. www.youtube.com/watch?v=xKPWngYf2Wk.

GirlScouts.org. "Traditions and Ceremonies," n.d. www.girlscouts.org/en/members/for-volunteers/traditions-and-ceremonies.html.

Glatter, Kathryn A., and Paul Finkelman. "History of the Plague: An Ancient Pandemic for the Age of COVID-19." *American Journal of Medicine* 134, no. 2 (February 2021): 176–81.

Goodman, Ryan, and Danielle Schulkin. "Timeline of the Coronavirus Pandemic and U.S. Response." Just Security, April 13, 2020. www.justsecurity.org/69650/timeline-of-the-coronavirus-pandemic-and-u-s-response/.

Grady, Denise. "Death at the Corners." *Discover*, January 18, 1993. www.discovermagazine.com/health/death-at-the-corners.

Guinan, Mary E., and Anne D. Mather. *Adventures of a Female Medical Detective: In Pursuit of Smallpox and AIDS*. Baltimore: Johns Hopkins University Press, 2016.

Gupta, Sanjay. "Lead Vaccine Developer Says She Wants to Help Rebuild Trust Brick by Brick." CNN, December 18, 2020. www.cnn.com/2020/12/16/health/kizzmekia-kizzy-corbett-interview-moderna-vaccine-gupta/index.html.

Hall, Jeffrey, E. "Health Equity Presentation, CDC Disease Detective Camp." Centers for Disease Control and Prevention, July 29, 2022.

Harden, Victoria Angela. *AIDS at 30: A History*. Washington, DC: Potomac Books, 2012.

Harper, David R., and Andrea S. Meyer. *Of Mice, Men, and Microbes: Hantavirus*. San Diego: Academic Press, 1999.

Hauser, Christine. "The Mask Slackers of 1918." *New York Times*, August 3, 2020. www.nytimes.com/2020/08/03/us/mask-protests-1918.html.

Haywood, Anne. "Amazon Deforestation and Climate Change." *National*

Geographic, March 11, 2024. education.nationalgeographic
.org/resource/amazon-deforestation-and-climate-change/.

Henderson, Donald A., and Richard Preston. *Smallpox: The Death of a Disease: The Inside Story of Eradicating a Worldwide Killer*. Guilford: Prometheus Books, 2021.

Herb, Jeremy, and Lauren Fox. "Fauci Tells Congress That States Face Serious Consequences If They Reopen Too Quickly." CNN, May 12, 2020. www.cnn.com/2020/05/12/politics/anthony-fauci -congress-hearing/index.html.

Higginbotham, Peter. "The Workhouse: The Story of an Institution . . ." n.d. www.workhouses.org.uk/intro/.

Highleyman, Liz. "First Person May Be Cured of HIV after Stem Cell Transplant without CCR5 Mutation." Aidsmap, July 20, 2023. www.aidsmap.com/news/jul-2023/first-person-may-be-cured-hiv -after-stem-cell-transplant-without-ccr5-mutation.

Hill, Latoya, and Samantha Artiga. "COVID-19 Cases and Deaths by Race/Ethnicity: Current Data and Changes Over Time." Kaiser Family Foundation, August 22, 2022. www.kff.org/racial-equity -and-health-policy/issue-brief/covid-19-cases-and-deaths-by-race -ethnicity-current-data-and-changes-over-time/.

HIV.gov. "A Timeline of HIV and AIDS." n.d. www.hiv.gov/hiv-basics /overview/history/hiv-and-aids-timeline.

HIV.gov Clinical Info. "Guidelines for the Prevention and Treatment of Opportunistic Infections in Adults and Adolescents with HIV." July 1, 2021. clinicalinfo.hiv.gov/en/guidelines/hiv-clinical-guidelines -adult-and-adolescent-opportunistic-infections/cytomegalovirus.

Hoffman, John, and Janet Tobias, dirs. *Fauci*. Magnolia Pictures, 2021. films.nationalgeographic.com/fauci.

Holmes, Eddie. "Eddie Holmes: De-Coding COVID-19." *Afternoons* (Radio New Zealand), February 17, 2021. www.rnz.co.nz/national /programmes/afternoons/audio/2018783995/eddie-holmes -de-coding-covid-19.

Honigsbaum, Mark. "Resurrecting the Killer." June 28, 2018, in *Going Viral—The Podcast*. podcasts.apple.com/gb/podcast/resurrecting -the-killer/id1396018157?i=1000414865125.

———. *The Pandemic Century: One Hundred Years of Panic, Hysteria, and Hubris*. First published as a Norton paperback. New York: W. W. Norton & Company, 2020.

Hopkins, Donald R. "Ramses V: Earliest Known Victim?" *World Health* (May 1980): 22–26. iris.who.int/handle/10665/202495.

Hoppe, Trevor. "'Spanish Flu': When Infectious Disease Names Blur Origins and Stigmatize Those Infected." *American Journal of Public Health* 108, no. 11 (November 2018): 1462–64. doi.org/10.2105/AJPH.2018.304645.

Hoyle, Rob. "Honoring mRNA Pioneers Katalin Karikó and Drew Weissman | 20-Minute Health Talk." Northwell Health. September 19, 2022. www.youtube.com/watch?v=r6E9Y_L8hks.

HRSA: Ryan White HIV/AIDS Program. "First Protease Inhibitor Becomes Available," n.d. ryanwhite.hrsa.gov/livinghistory/1995.

———. "Thirty Years of Innovating Care, Optimizing Public Health, Ending the HIV Epidemic." n.d. ryanwhite.hrsa.gov/livinghistory/.

Hubbard, Jim, dir. *United in Anger: A History of ACT UP.* New York State Council on the Arts, 2012.

Hunt, David M., Kanwaijit S. Dulai, James K. Bowmaker, and John D. Mollon. "The Chemistry of John Dalton's Color Blindness." *Science* 267, no. 5200 (February 17, 1995): 984–88. doi.org/10.1126/science.7863342.

Hutton, Belle. "Remembering Larry Kramer Through His Most Powerful Words." *AnOther Magazine*, May 28, 2020. www.anothermag.com/design-living/12559/remembering-larry-kramer-quotes-act-up-writer-aids-activist-new-york.

Haynes, Benjamin, and Nancy E. Messonnier. "CDC Media Telebriefing: Update on COVID-19." February 26, 2020. stacks.cdc.gov/view/cdc/85310.

"Inside the Lab That Invented the COVID-19 Vaccine." Be Smart, December 8, 2020. www.youtube.com/watch?v=-92HQA0GcI8&t=1s.

Iwry, Jonathan. "From 9/11 to COVID-19: A Brief History of FDA Emergency Use Authorization." *Bill of Health* (blog), January 28, 2021. blog.petrieflom.law.harvard.edu/2021/01/28/fda-emergency-use-authorization-history/.

Jackson, Lisa A., Evan J. Anderson, Nadine G. Rouphael, Paul C. Roberts, Mamodikoe Makhene, Rhea N. Coler, Michele P. McCullough, et al. "An mRNA Vaccine against SARS-CoV-2—Preliminary Report." *New England Journal of Medicine* 383, no. 20 (November 12, 2020): 1920–31. doi.org/10.1056/NEJMoa2022483.

Jenson, Deborah. "Thank This Ebola-Fighting African Doctor for Monoclonal Antibody Treatments." StatNews.com, October 15, 2020. www.statnews.com/2020/10/15/thank-this-ebola-fighting-african-doctor-muyembe-tamfum-for-monoclonal-antibody-treatments/.

Jeung, Russell, Tara Popovic, Richard Lim, and Nelson Lin. "Anti-Chinese Rhetoric Employed by Perpetrators of Anti-Asian Hate." Stop AAPI Hate. October 11, 2020. stopaapihate.org/wp-content /uploads/2021/04/Stop-AAPI-Hate-Report-Anti-China-201011.pdf.

Johnson, Carolyn Y. "A One-Way Ticket. A Cash-Stuffed Teddy Bear. A Dream Decades in the Making." *Washington Post*. October 1, 2021. www.washingtonpost.com/health/2021/10/01/katalin -kariko-covid-vaccines/.

Johnson, Steven. *The Ghost Map: The Story of London's Most Terrifying Epidemic—and How It Changed Science, Cities, and the Modern World*. New York: Riverhead, 2007.

Jordan, Douglas. "The Deadliest Flu: The Complete Story of the Discovery and Reconstruction of the 1918 Pandemic Virus," December 17, 2019. archive.cdc.gov/#/details?url=https://www.cdc .gov/flu/pandemic-resources/reconstruction-1918-virus.html.

Kahn, Jennifer. "The Disease Detective." *New York Times*, June 3, 2021, sec. Magazine. www.nytimes.com/2021/06/03/magazine /metagenomic-sequencing.html.

Kanamine, Linda. "Navajo Flu Claims 11." *USA Today*. June 1, 1993. 1A. Newsbank.

Kane, Andrea. "The First Phase 3 Coronavirus Vaccine Trial in the US Is Expected to Begin Next Week. Here's How the Vaccine Works." *Philadelphia Tribune*, September 2, 2020. www .phillytrib.com/news/health/coronavirus/the-first-phase-3 -coronavirus-vaccine-trial-in-the-us-is-expected-to-begin-next /article_88297832-d00a-11ea-a9b2-57b419e0d9ad.html.

Karikó, Katalin, and Drew Weissman. "The Story Behind mRNA COVID Vaccines: Katalin Karikó and Drew Weissman." Penn Medicine, September 24, 2021. www.youtube.com /watch?v=DyCmhKMd148.

Klenerman, Paul. *The Immune System: A Very Short Introduction*. Oxford: Oxford University Press, 2017.

Kolata, Gina. "AIDS Researcher Seeks Wide Access to Drugs in Tests." *New York Times*, June 26, 1989, sec. A. timesmachine.nytimes .com/timesmachine/1989/06/26/097989.html?pageNumber=1.

———. "FDA Approves the Use of an Experimental Drug for AIDS Patients' Eye Infections." *New York Times*, March 3, 1989, sec. A. www.nytimes.com/1989/03/03/us/fda-approves-the-use-of-an -experimental-drug-for-aids-patients-eye-infections.html.

————. "FDA Said to Be Re-Evaluating Order for More Studies on an AIDS Drug." *New York Times*, February 6, 1989, sec. B. timesmachine.nytimes.com/timesmachine/1989/02/06/203089.html.

————. *Flu: The Story of the Great Influenza Pandemic of 1918 and the Search for the Virus That Caused It*. New York: Farrar, Straus and Giroux, 2011.

————. "Long Overlooked, Kati Karikó Helped Shield the World from the Coronavirus." *New York Times*. April 8, 2021. www.nytimes.com/2021/04/08/health/coronavirus-mrna-kariko.html.

Kolata, Gina, and Benjamin Mueller. "Halting Progress and Happy Accidents: How mRNA Vaccines Were Made." *New York Times*, January 15, 2022. www.nytimes.com/2022/01/15/health/mrna-vaccine.html.

Kozlowski, Diego, Vincent Larivière, Cassidy R. Sugimoto, and Thema Monroe-White. "Intersectional Inequalities in Science." *Proceedings of the National Academy of Sciences* 119, no. 2 (January 4, 2022). doi.org/10.1073/pnas.2113067119.

Kramer, Jillian. "They Spent 12 Years Solving a Puzzle. It Yielded the First COVID-19 Vaccines." *National Geographic*, December 31, 2020. www.nationalgeographic.com/science/article/these-scientists-spent-twelve-years-solving-puzzle-yielded-coronavirus-vaccines?loggedin=true&rnd=1669932933102.

Kramer, Larry. "1,112 and Counting." *New York Native*, March 14, 1983. calisphere.org/item/c3ac821c-4caa-4b33-a25d-1ac7c2adc4cc/.

Krellenstein, James, Aaron Lord, and Peter Staley. "Why Don't More Americans Use PrEP?" *New York Times*, July 16, 2018, New York edition, sec. A. www.nytimes.com/2018/07/16/opinion/prep-hiv-aids-drug.html.

Laden, Lisa, dir. *We Heard the Bells: The Influenza of 1918*. US Department of Health and Human Services, January 2010. www.youtube.com/watch?v=XbEefT_M6xY.

Lalla, Nadia J., and Marie Boissière. "Smallpox Eradication in India, 1972–1977." University of Michigan Library, n.d. apps.lib.umich.edu/online-exhibits/exhibits/show/smallpox-eradication-india.

Langmuir, Alexander D. "The Epidemic Intelligence Service of the Center for Disease Control." *Public Health Reports (1974—)* 95, no. 5 (1980): 470–477. www.jstor.org/stable/4596361.

Larson, Erik. "The Flu Hunters." *Time*, February 23, 1998. content.time.com/time/subscriber/article/0,33009,987857,00.html.

Leary, Warren E. "FDA Pressed to Approve More AIDS Drugs." *New York Times*, October 11, 1988, sec. C, www.nytimes .com/1988/10/11/science/fda-pressed-to-approve-more-aids-drugs .html.

Levenson, Michael. "Scale of China's Wuhan Shutdown Is Believed to Be Without Precedent." *New York Times*, January 22, 2020. www .nytimes.com/2020/01/22/world/asia/coronavirus-quarantines -history.html.

Levitt, Alexandra M. *Deadly Outbreaks: How Medical Detectives Save Lives Threatened by Killer Pandemics, Exotic Viruses, and Drug-Resistant Parasites.* New York: Skyhorse, 2015.

Littman, Robert J. "The Plague of Athens: Epidemiology and Paleopathology." *Mount Sinai Journal of Medicine: A Journal of Translational and Personalized Medicine* 76, no. 5 (September 28, 2009): 456–67. doi.org/10.1002/msj.20137.

Mark, Joshua J. "Thucydides on the Plague of Athens: Text and Commentary." World History Encyclopedia, April 1, 2020. www .worldhistory.org/article/1535/thucydides-on-the-plague-of-athens -text—commentar/.

Markel, Howard. "Will the Largest Quarantine in History Just Make Things Worse?" *New York Times*, January 27, 2020. www.nytimes .com/2020/01/27/opinion/china-wuhan-virus-quarantine.html.

Maxmen, Amy. "Why Did the World's Pandemic Warning System Fail When COVID Hit?" *Nature*, January 23, 2021. www.nature.com /articles/d41586-021-00162-4.

Mayo Clinic Staff. "Cholera." December 9, 2022. www.mayoclinic.org /diseases-conditions/cholera/symptoms-causes/syc-20355287.

———. "Flu Shot: Your Best Bet for Avoiding Influenza." September 22, 2023. www.mayoclinic.org/diseases-conditions/flu/in-depth/flu -shots/art-20048000.

McLellan, Dennis. "Ernest Hendon, 96; Tuskegee Syphilis Study's Last Survivor." *Los Angeles Times*, January 25, 2004. www.latimes .com/archives/la-xpm-2004-jan-25-me-hendon25-story.html.

McCormick, Joseph B., Susan Fisher-Hoch, and Leslie Alan Horvitz. *Level 4: Virus Hunters of the CDC.* New York: Barnes & Noble Books, 1999.

McKenna, Maryn. *Beating Back the Devil: On the Front Lines with the Disease Detectives of the Epidemic Intelligence Service.* New York: Free Press, 2004.

McMillen, Christian W. *Pandemics: A Very Short Introduction*. New York: Oxford University Press, 2016.

McKnight, Michael. "Into the Wild. Twice. For Mankind." *Sports Illustrated*, May 27, 2020. www.si.com/more-sports/2020/05/27 /johan-hultin-the-virus-hunter.

McMurry, Michelle. "The Elephant in the Room: What about HIV?" *I Am Bio* (blog), September 14, 2021. www.biotech-now.org/blogs /elephant-room-what-about-hiv.

Mendoza, Jean, Debbie Reese, and Roxanne Dunbar-Ortiz. *An Indigenous Peoples' History of the United States for Young People*. Boston: Beacon Press, 2019.

Moderna. "The Power of mRNA." n.d. www.modernatx.com/en-US /power-of-mrna/science-of-mrna.

Moderna, Inc. "United States Securities and Exchange Commission, Form 10-K." December 31, 2018. www.sec.gov/Archives/edgar /data/1682852/000168285219000009/moderna10-k12312018.htm.

Morales, Laurel. "For the Navajo Nation, Uranium Mining's Deadly Legacy Lingers." NPR, April 10, 2016. www.npr.org/sections /health-shots/2016/04/10/473547227/for-the-navajo-nation -uranium-minings-deadly-legacy-lingers.

Morens, David M., Jeffery K. Taubenberger, and Anthony S. Fauci. "Predominant Role of Bacterial Pneumonia as a Cause of Death in Pandemic Influenza: Implications for Pandemic Influenza Preparedness." *Journal of Infectious Diseases* 198, no. 7 (October 2008): 962–70. doi.org/10.1086/591708.

Mudgal, Mukesh M., Nagaraju Birudukota, and Mayur A. Doke. "Applications of Click Chemistry in the Development of HIV Protease Inhibitors." *International Journal of Medicinal Chemistry* 2018 (July 2018): 1–9.

Nair, Prashant. "QnAs with Katalin Karikó." *Proceedings of the National Academy of Sciences* 118, no. 51 (December 13, 2021). doi.org/10.1073/pnas.2119757118.

Nall, Rachel. "How Does HIV Affect the Body?" Healthline, April 24, 2020. www.healthline.com/health/hiv-aids/how-hiv-affects-the -body.

National Institute of Allergy and Infectious Diseases. "Anthony S. Fauci, M.D." September 29, 2021. www.niaid.nih.gov/about /anthony-s-fauci-md-bio.

———. "Vaccine Research Center Brochure." NIAID Vaccine Research

Center, November 2018. NIH Publication No. 18-AI-8048.

National Institute on Minority Health and Health Disparities.
"Diversity and Inclusion in Clinical Trials," January 12, 2024.
www.nimhd.nih.gov/resources/understanding-health-disparities
/diversity-and-inclusion-in-clinical-trials.html.

National Library of Medicine. "1864: The Navajos Begin 'Long Walk'
to Imprisonment." n.d. www.nlm.nih.gov/nativevoices
/timeline/332.html.

———. "Reports of the Surgeon General: The AIDS Epidemic." n.d.
profiles.nlm.nih.gov/spotlight/nn/feature/aids.

National Museum of Health and Medicine. "Closing in on a Killer:
Scientists Unlock Clues to the Spanish Influenza Virus."
December 5, 2017. medicalmuseum.health.mil/index.cfm?p=visit
.exhibits.virtual.1918killerflu.index.

NBC News. "Trump Administration Declares Coronavirus a Public
Health Emergency." January 31, 2020. www.nbcnews.com/video
/trump-administration-declares-coronavirus-a-public-health
-emergency-77905989990.

New Mexico Department of Health. "Department of Health Reports
Sixth Hantavirus Case of 2023." June 21, 2023. www.nmhealth
.org/news/alert/2023/6/?view=1973.

New York Times Staff. "C.D.C. Recommends Wearing Masks in Public;
Trump Says, 'I'm Choosing Not to Do It.'" *New York Times*,
April 3, 2020, sec. World. www.nytimes.com/2020/04/03/world
/coronavirus-news-updates.html.

Nguyen, Kimberly H., Anup Srivastav, Hilda Razzaghi, Walter
Williams, Megan C. Lindley, Cynthia Jorgensen, Neetu Abad, and
James A. Singleton. "COVID-19 Vaccination Intent, Perceptions,
and Reasons for Not Vaccinating Among Groups Prioritized for
Early Vaccination—United States, September and December 2020."
Morbidity and Mortality Weekly Report 70, no. 6 (February 12,
2021): 217–22. doi.org/10.15585/mmwr.mm7006e3.

Nichols, E., and Institute of Medicine (US) Roundtable for the
Development of Drugs and Vaccines Against AIDS. *Expanding
Access to Investigational Therapies for HIV Infection and AIDS:
March 12–13, 1990 Conference Summary*. Washington, DC:
National Academies Press, 1991. www.ncbi.nlm.nih.gov/books
/NBK234129/.

O'Gan, Patri. "Victory at Home and Abroad: African American Army
Nurses in World War II." National Museum of African American

History & Culture, May 8, 2023. nmaahc.si.edu/explore/stories /nurses-WWII.

Office of Disease Prevention and Health Promotion. "HIV Workgroup." n.d. health.gov/healthypeople/about/workgroups/hiv-workgroup.

Pallesen, Jesper, Nianshuang Wang, Kizzmekia S. Corbett, Daniel Wrapp, Robert N. Kirchdoerfer, Hannah L. Turner, Christopher A. Cottrell, et al. "Immunogenicity and Structures of a Rationally Designed Prefusion MERS-CoV Spike Antigen." *Proceedings of the National Academy of Sciences* 114, no. 35 (August 14, 2017). doi.org/10.1073/pnas.1707304114.

Park, Alice, and Jamie Ducharme. "The Miracle Workers." *Time*, December 13, 2021. time.com/heroes-of-the-year-2021-vaccine -scientists/.

Pellowski, Jennifer A., Seth C. Kalichman, Karen A. Matthews, and Nancy Adler. "A Pandemic of the Poor: Social Disadvantage and the U.S. HIV Epidemic." *American Psychologist* 68, no. 4 (May–June 2013): 197–209.

Pendergrast, Mark. *Inside the Outbreaks: The Elite Medical Detectives of the Epidemic Intelligence Service.* Boston: Houghton Mifflin Harcourt, 2010.

Peters, C. J., and Mark Olshaker. *Virus Hunter: Thirty Years of Battling Hot Viruses Around the World.* New York: Anchor Books, 1997.

Pfizer. "Biopharma Leaders Unite to Stand with Science." September 8, 2020. www.pfizer.com/news/press-release/press-release-detail /biopharma-leaders-unite-stand-science.

———. "Pfizer and BioNTech to Co-Develop Potential COVID-19 Vaccine." March 17, 2020. investors.pfizer.com/Investors/News /news-details/2020/Pfizer-and-BioNTech-to-Co-Develop-Potential -COVID-19-Vaccine-03-17-2020/default.aspx.

———. "Pfizer and BioNTech Announce Vaccine Candidate Against COVID-19 Achieved Success in First Interim Analysis from Phase 3 Study." November 9, 2020. www.pfizer.com/news/press-release /press-release-detail/pfizer-and-biontech-announce-vaccine -candidate-against.

———. "Inside a Cytokine Storm: When Your Immune System Is Too Strong." n.d. www.pfizer.com/news/articles/inside_a_cytokine _storm_when_your_immune_system_is_too_strong.

Preston, Richard. *The Demon in the Freezer.* New York: Random House, 2002.

Racaniello, Vincent. "This Week in Virology: 1918 Influenza with

Jeffery Taubenberger." MicrobeTV, December 23, 2022. www
.youtube.com/watch?v=uRgS4BNRNuU.

Reid, Ann H., Thomas G. Fanning, Johan V. Hultin, and Jeffery
K. Taubenberger. "Origin and Evolution of the 1918 'Spanish'
Influenza Virus Hemagglutinin Gene." *Proceedings of the National
Academy of Sciences* 96, no. 4 (February 16, 1999): 1651–56.
doi.org/10.1073/pnas.96.4.1651.

Reuters Staff. "China Coronavirus Deaths Rise 254 to 1,367 at End-
Feb 12." Reuters, February 13, 2020. www.reuters.com/article
/us-china-health-toll/china-coronavirus-deaths-rise-254-to-1367-at
-end-feb-12-idUSKBN2070UN.

Reyes, Cecilia, Nausheen Husain, Christy Gutowski, Stacy St. Clair,
and Gregory Royal Pratt. "Chicago's Coronavirus Disparity: Black
Chicagoans Are Dying at Nearly Six Times the Rate of White
Residents, Data Show." *Chicago Tribune*, April 7, 2020.
www.chicagotribune.com/coronavirus/ct-coronavirus-chicago
-coronavirus-deaths-demographics-lightfoot-20200406
-77nlylhiavgjzb2wa4ckivh7mu-story.html.

Rid, Annette, Marc Lipsitch, and Franklin G. Miller. "The Ethics
of Continuing Placebo in SARS-CoV-2 Vaccine Trials." JAMA
Network, December 14, 2020. jamanetwork.com/journals/jama
/fullarticle/2774382.

Riedel, Stefan. "Edward Jenner and the History of Smallpox and
Vaccination." *Baylor University Medical Center Proceedings* 18,
no. 1 (January 2005): 21–25. doi.org/10.1080/08998280.2005
.11928028.

Robbins, Michael W. "The First Wave: Remembering the Influenza
Pandemic of 1918–19." *American Scholar*, April 23, 2020.
theamericanscholar.org/the-first-wave/.

Roberts, Joanna. "Five Things You Need to Know About: mRNA
Vaccines." *Horizon: The EU Research & Innovation Magazine*,
April 1, 2020. ec.europa.eu/research-and-innovation/en/horizon
-magazine/five-things-you-need-know-about-mrna-vaccines.

Roberts, William. "Facts and Ideas from Anywhere." *Baylor University
Medical Center Proceedings* 32, no. 3 (June 19, 2019): 468–76.
doi.org/10.1080/08998280.2019.1619423.

Robson, David. "Why the Flu of 1918 Was So Deadly." BBC, October
30, 2018. www.bbc.com/future/article/20181029-why-the-flu-of
-1918-was-so-deadly.

Roos, Robert. "NIH Panel Supports Stronger Safeguards for H5N1
Research." *Center for Infectious Disease Research and Policy*
(blog), January 25, 2013. www.cidrap.umn.edu/avian-influenza
-bird-flu/nih-panel-supports-stronger-safeguards-h5n1-research.

Rosenwald, Michael S. "Suffering from Smallpox after Gettysburg,
Lincoln May Have Infected His Valet." *Washington Post*, October
11, 2020, sec. Retropolis. www.washingtonpost.com
/history/2020/10/11/lincoln-smallpox-valet-died/.

Ross, Janell. "Meet Kizzmekia Corbett, the 34-Year-Old Scientist
Developing a Vaccine for Coronavirus." *Today*, April 15, 2020, sec.
Health. www.today.com/tmrw/kizzmekia-corbett-scientist
-developing-coronavirus-vaccine-t178661?cid=public-rss_20200417.

Rummler, Orion. "U.S. Set to End 2020 with Just Over 3 Million
Vaccine Doses Administered." Axios, December 31, 2020. www
.axios.com/2020/12/31/coronavirus-vaccines-administered-2020.

Russo, Vito. "Why We Fight" (speech), 1988. NYPL Tape #1723. ACT
UP Oral History Project. actuporalhistory.org/actions/seize-control
-of-the-fda.

Saracci, Rodolfo. *Epidemiology: A Very Short Introduction*. Oxford;
New York: Oxford University Press, 2010.

Schellekens, Philip. "Mapping Our Unvaccinated World." Panedem[ic],
April 6, 2024. pandem-ic.com/mapping-our-unvaccinated-world/.
———. "The Unfinished Business of COVID-19 Vaccination."
Pandem[ic]. April 6, 2024. pandem-ic.com/the-unfinished-business
-of-covid-19-vaccination/.

Schulman, Sarah. *Let the Record Show: A Political History of ACT
UP New York, 1987–1993*. New York: Farrar, Straus and Giroux,
2021.

Scott, Dylan, and Christina Animashaun. "COVID-19's Stunning
Unequal Death Toll in America, in One Chart." Vox, October 2,
2020. www.vox.com/coronavirus-covid19/2020/10/2/21496884
/us-covid-19-deaths-by-race-black-white-americans.

Shah, Sonia. *Pandemic: Tracking Contagions, from Cholera to Ebola
and Beyond*. New York: Picador, 2017.

Shapiro, Lucy, and Richard Losick. "Delivering the Message: How a
Novel Technology Enabled the Rapid Development of Effective
Vaccines." *Cell* 184, no. 21 (October 2021): 5271–74.
doi.org/10.1016/j.cell.2021.08.019.

Sharfstein, Dr. Joshua M. "1988 AIDS Protest at the FDA." Johns

Hopkins Bloomberg School of Public Health, Baltimore, October 11, 2018. www.c-span.org/video/?452831-1/1988-aids-protest-fda.

———. *The Public Health Crisis Survival Guide: Leadership and Management in Trying Times*. New York: Oxford University Press, 2018.

Simon, Scott. "'I Wanted to Do Something,' Says Mother of Two Who Is First to Test Coronavirus Vaccine." NPR, March 21, 2020. www.npr.org/transcripts/818759617.

Skarland, Ivar. "Otto William Geist, 1888–1963." *American Antiquity* 29, no. 4 (April 1964): 484–85. doi.org/10.1017/S0002731600014050.

Slack, Paul. *Plague: A Very Short Introduction*. New York: Oxford University Press, 2012.

Snow, John. *On the Mode of Communication of Cholera*. 2nd ed. London: John Churchill, 1855.

Sowards, Will. "How the 1918 Spanish Flu Pandemic Links to World War I." *Passport Health* (blog), April 13, 2020. www.passporthealthusa.com/2020/04/1918-spanish-flu-links-to-world-war-i/.

Staley, Peter. "Anthony Fauci Quietly Shocked Us All." *New York Times*, December 31, 2022. www.nytimes.com/2022/12/31/opinion/anthony-fauci-hiv-aids-act-up.html?searchResultPosition=1.

———. *Never Silent: ACT UP and My Life in Activism*. Chicago: Chicago Review Press, 2021.

———. "Peter Staley Speech at the Sixth International Conference on AIDS." San Francisco, June 20, 1990. www.youtube.com/watch?v=Vn8qEjPnoSo.

Sternberg, S. "A Doughboy's Lungs Yield 1918 Flu Virus." *Science News* 151, no.12 (March 22, 1997): 172.

———. "An Outbreak of Pain." *USA Today*, July 2, 1998, sec. Life.

———. "Rodent Virus Attack Not as Severe in '98." *USA Today*, January 19, 1999, sec. Life.

———. "Science, Legwork Combine to Catch Deadly Virus." *USA Today*, July 6, 1998. Westlaw.

———." Tracking a Mysterious Killer Virus in the Southwest." *Washington Post*, June 14, 1994. Westlaw.

Sternlicht, Alexandra. "Fauci: 'We Might Have a Vaccine by the End of the Year.'" *Forbes*, May 27, 2020. www.forbes.com/sites/alexandrasternlicht/2020/05/27/fauci-we-might-have-a-vaccine-by-the-end-of-the-year/?sh=4a7bb4176043.

Sturner, Stacey. "1918 Flu & COVID-19: A Tale of Two Pandemics."

Each Breath (blog), May 19, 2020. www.lung.org/blog/flu-covid-two-pandemics.

Subbaraman, Nidhi. "This COVID-Vaccine Designer Is Tackling Vaccine Hesitancy—in Churches and on Twitter." *Nature* 590, no. 7846 (February 11, 2021): 377. doi.org/10.1038/d41586-021-00338-y.

Summers, Juana. "Timeline: How Trump Has Downplayed the Coronavirus Pandemic." NPR, October 2, 2020. www.npr.org/sections/latest-updates-trump-covid-19-results/2020/10/02/919432383/how-trump-has-downplayed-the-coronavirus-pandemic.

Tanner, Lindsey. "First COVID-19 Shot Recipient in US Now a Vaccine Activist." *U.S. News & World Report,* December 28, 2021. www.usnews.com/news/health-news/articles/2021-12-28/first-covid-19-shot-recipient-in-us-now-a-vaccine-activist.

Taubenberger, Jeffery K., Ann H. Reid, Amy E. Krafft, Karen E. Bijwaard, and Thomas G. Fanning. "Initial Genetic Characterization of the 1918 'Spanish' Influenza Virus." *Science* 275, no. 5307 (March 21, 1997): 1793–96. doi.org/10.1126/science.275.5307.1793.

Taubenberger, Jeffery K. "Sanger Series: 'Going Viral' Featuring Jeffery K. Taubenberger." VCU Libraries, February 19, 2018. www.youtube.com/watch?v=QAWtOBnPavA.

———. "Why Study the 1918 Influenza Pandemic?" National Institute of Allergy and Infectious Diseases (NIAID), October 18, 2018. www.youtube.com/watch?v=O40IeoUp6u8.

Thaczuk, Derek. "AZT (Zidovudine, Retrovir)." Canada AIDS Treatment Information Exchange, 2014. www.catie.ca/azt-zidovudine-retrovir.

The Foundation for AIDS Research (amfAR). "Snapshots of an Epidemic: An HIV/AIDS Timeline," n.d. www.amfar.org/about-hiv-aids/snapshots-of-an-epidemic-hiv-aids/.

The Franklin Institute. "Kizzmekia Corbett." March 2021. www.fi.edu/laureates/kizzmekia-s-corbett.

The Vaccine: Conquering COVID. Glass Entertainment Group, 2021.

Tucker, Eric, Zeke Miller, and Mike Schneider. "Face Coverings Recommended, but Trump Says He Won't Wear One." *AP News,* April 4, 2020. apnews.com/article/health-donald-trump-ap-top-news-virus-outbreak-understanding-the-outbreak-227fa2d005b3923157b9eb736c12e6c5.

Tumpey, Terrance M. "Genetically Engineering the Avian Flu." By Chad Cohen. NOVA scienceNOW, PBS, (2009). pbsnc.pbslearningmedia .org/resource/biot09.biotech.tools.avianflu/genetically-engineering -the-avian-flu/.

Tumpey, Terrence M., Christopher F. Basler, Patricia V. Aguilar, Hui Zeng, Alicia Solórzano, David E. Swayne, Nancy J. Cox, et al. "Characterization of the Reconstructed 1918 Spanish Influenza Pandemic Virus." *Science* 310, no. 5745 (October 7, 2005): 77–80. doi.org/10.1126/science.1119392.

United Nations. "Over 1 Billion in 43 Nations at Risk Amid Cholera Outbreaks, WHO Says." February 25, 2023. news.un.org/en /story/2023/02/1133907.

US Department of Health and Human Services. "Explaining Operation Warp Speed." n.d. www.nihb.org/covid-19/wp-content /uploads/2020/08/Fact-sheet-operation-warp-speed.pdf.

———. "Update on the New Coronavirus Outbreak First Identified in Wuhan, China." January 28, 2020. www.youtube.com/embed /w6koHkBCoNQ?rel=0.

US Department of Labor. "Americans with Disabilities Act." n.d. www.dol.gov/general/topic/disability/ada.

US Food & Drug Administration. "Treatment Use of Investigational Drugs: Guidance for Institutional Review Boards and Clinical Investigators." FDA: Office of the Commissioner, Office of Clinical Policy and Programs, Office of Clinical Policy, Office of Good Clinical Practice, January 1998. public4.pagefreezer.com /content/FDA/01-02-2023T10:30/https://www.fda.gov/regulatory -information/search-fda-guidance-documents/treatment-use -investigational-drugs.

Vaid, Urvashi. "Critics of President George H. W. Bush Reflect on His Handling of the AIDS Crisis." By Ailsa Chang. *All Things Considered* (NPR). December 4, 2018. www.npr.org/2018 /12/04/673398013/critics-of-president-george-h-w-bush-reflect -on-his-handling-of-the-aids-crisis.

Van Hook, Charles J. "Hantavirus Pulmonary Syndrome—The 25th Anniversary of the Four Corners Outbreak." *Emerging Infectious Diseases* 24, no. 11 (November 2018): 2056–60. wwwnc.cdc.gov /eid/article/24/11/18-0381_article.

Vazquez, Marietta. "Calling COVID-19 the 'Wuhan Virus' or 'China Virus' Is Inaccurate and Xenophobic." Yale School of Medicine,

March 12, 2020. medicine.yale.edu/news-article/calling-covid-19 -the-wuhan-virus-or-china-virus-is-inaccurate-and-xenophobic/.

Vinten-Johansen, Peter, ed. *Cholera, Chloroform, and the Science of Medicine: A Life of John Snow.* Oxford; New York: Oxford University Press, 2003.

Vora, Neil, et al. "Interventions to Reduce Risk of Pathogen Spillover and Early Disease Spread to Prevent Outbreaks, Epidemics, and Pandemics." *Emerging Infectious Diseases* 29, no. 3 (March 2023): 1–9. doi.org/10.3201/eid2903.221079.

Vora, Neil M., Yu Li, Marika Geleishvili, Ginny L. Emerson, Ekaterine Khmaladze, Giorgi Maghlakelidze, Archil Navdarashvili, et al. "Human Infection with a Zoonotic Orthopoxvirus in the Country of Georgia." *New England Journal of Medicine* 372, no. 13 (March 26, 2015): 1223–30. doi.org/10.1056/NEJMoa1407647.

Wayne, Marta L., and Benjamin M. Bolker. *Infectious Disease: A Very Short Introduction.* Oxford: Oxford University Press, 2015.

Weinraub, Bernard. "Reagan Hears AIDS Has No. 1 Priority." *New York Times*, December 20, 1985, sec. A. www.nytimes .com/1985/12/20/us/reagan-hears-aids-has-no-1-priority.html.

World Health Organization (WHO). "Cholera: Global Situation." Disease Outbreak News, December 16, 2022. www.who.int /emergencies/disease-outbreak-news/item/2022-DON426.

———. "Cholera: Global Situation." Disease Outbreak News, February 11, 2023. www.who.int/emergencies/disease-outbreak-news /item/2023-DON437.

———. "Coronavirus Disease (COVID-19): Vaccines and Vaccine Safety." December 5, 2023. www.who.int/news-room/questions -and-answers/item/coronavirus-disease-(covid-19)-vaccines.

———. "COVID-19 Vaccines." November 29, 2021. healthalert .whofreebasics.org/sections/your-questions-answered/vaccines-and -immunization-what-vaccination/.

———. "The Global Eradication of Smallpox: Final Report of the Global Commission for the Certification of Smallpox Eradication." Geneva, Switzerland, 1979. iris.who.int/handle/10665/39253.

———. "MERS Situation Update, October 2022." World Health Organization, Regional Office for the Eastern Mediterranean, October 2022. applications.emro.who.int/docs/WHOEMCSR579E -eng.pdf?ua=1.

———. "Multi-Country Outbreak of Mpox, External Situation Report

#27." August 14, 2023. https://www.who.int/publications/m/item/multi-country-outbreak-of-mpox--external-situation-report-27---14-august-2023.

———. "Severe Acute Respiratory Syndrome (SARS)." n.d. www.who.int/health-topics/severe-acute-respiratory-syndrome#tab=tab_3.

Worobey, Michael, Joshua I. Levy, Lorena Malpica Serrano, Alexander Crits-Christoph, Jonathan E. Pekar, Stephen A. Goldstein, Angela L. Rasmussen, et al. "The Huanan Seafood Wholesale Market in Wuhan Was the Early Epicenter of the COVID-19 Pandemic." *Science* 377, no. 6609 (July 26, 2022): 951–59. doi.org/10.1126/science.abp8715.

Wright, Lawrence. "The Plague Year." *New Yorker*, December 28, 2020. www.newyorker.com/magazine/2021/01/04/the-plague-year.

Yan, Holly. "Here's Where We Stand on Getting a Coronavirus Vaccine." CNN, June 8, 2020, sec. Health. www.cnn.com/2020/06/08/health/covid-19-vaccine-latest/index.html.

Yeung, Jessie. "The US keeps millions of chickens in secret farms to make flu vaccines. But their eggs won't work for coronavirus." CNN, March 29, 2020. www.cnn.com/2020/03/27/health/chicken-egg-flu-vaccine-intl-hnk-scli/index.html.

Yu, Ting. "How Scientists Drew Weissman (MED'87, GRS'87) and Katalin Karikó Developed the Revolutionary mRNA Technology inside COVID Vaccines." *Bostonia*, November 18, 2021. www.bu.edu/articles/2021/how-drew-weissman-and-katalin-kariko-developed-mrna-technology-inside-covid-vaccines/.

Zimmer, Carl. "U.S. Is Blind to Contagious New Virus Variant, Scientists Warn." *New York Times*, January 6, 2021, sec. Health. www.nytimes.com/2021/01/06/health/coronavirus-variant-tracking.html.

Zuckerman, Gregory. *A Shot to Save the World: The Inside Story of the Life-or-Death Race for a Covid-19 Vaccine.* New York: Penguin Random House, 2021.

ENDNOTES

PART I: THE CASE OF THE NO-NAME VIRUS

Chapter 1
Page 7: Jay Butler describes the day he was chosen to lead the hantavirus outbreak investigation: Butler and Childs, "Of Mice and Men: Discovering a Deadly Hantavirus in the Americas."

Chapter 2
Page 11: Richard Malone's investigation of Merrill Bahe's and Florena Woody's deaths described: Sternberg, "Science, Legwork Combine to Catch Deadly Virus"; Grady, "Death at the Corners"; Van Hook, "Hantavirus Pulmonary Syndrome—The 25th Anniversary of the Four Corners Outbreak."

Page 12: Merrill Bahe and Florena Woody's courtship described: Sternberg, "An Outbreak of Pain."

Page 13: The next day . . . fluid: Levitt, *Deadly Outbreaks*, 162; Grady, "Death at the Corners."

Page 13: The days leading up to the death of Merrill Bahe and details of his last hours: Sternberg, "An Outbreak of Pain"; Grady, "Death at the Corners."

Page 15: Transmission of plague: Centers for Disease Control and Prevention, "Plague: Ecology and Transmission."

Page 15: Twenty-five million people died: Glatter and Finkelman, "History of the Plague: An Ancient Pandemic for the Age of COVID-19."

Page 15: Autopsies of Bahe and Woody by Patricia McFeeley: Sternberg, "An Outbreak of Pain"; Grady, "Death at the Corners."

Page 15: Every year, between . . . in the US: Centers for Disease Control and Prevention, "Plague: Frequently Asked Questions."

Page 15: "Why aren't we . . . out?": *Forensic Files*, season 4, episode 12, "With Every Breath," aired December 22, 1999.

Chapter 3

Page 17: "The agency provides . . . system.": Dr. James Cheek, interview with the author, August 23, 2022.

Page 17: Dr. James Cheek's inspection of the home of Merrill Bahe and Florena Woody's home: Dr. James Cheek, interview with the author, August 23, 2022.

Page 18: mortality rate of 75 percent: Van Hook, "Hantavirus Pulmonary Syndrome—The 25th Anniversary of the Four Corners Outbreak," 2058.

Page 18: at least eight people were dead: Cole, "Mystery Flu Death Toll at 8."

Chapter 4

Page 19: "Navajo Flu Claims 11": Kanamine, "Navajo Flu Claims 11."

Page 20: The Long Walk described: Bruchac, *Navajo Long Walk*, 25–38; National Library of Medicine, "1864: The Navajos Begin 'Long Walk' to Imprisonment."

Page 20: marched them 470 miles: Bruchac, *Navajo Long Walk*, 25.

Page 20: at least 8,500 Diné and 500 Ndé: National Library of Medicine, "1864: The Navajos Begin 'Long Walk' to Imprisonment."

Page 20: "military concentration camp . . . Redondo.": Mendoza, Reese, and Dunbar-Ortiz, *An Indigenous Peoples' History of the United States for Young People*, 141–142.

Chapter 5

Page 21: CDC's deployment to the Four Corners Outbreak described: Sternberg, "Science, Legwork Combine to Catch Deadly Virus"; Grady, "Death at the Corners."

Page 22: Later that night . . . gloves: Levitt, *Deadly Outbreaks*, 165.

Page 22: "There's this sense . . . you.": Sternberg, "Science, Legwork Combine to Catch Deadly Virus."

Chapter 6

Page 23: "a very simple . . . 1993.": Butler and Childs, "Of Mice and Men: Discovering a Deadly Hantavirus in the Americas."

Page 24: Task force meeting described: Butler and Childs, "Of Mice and Men: Discovering a Deadly Hantavirus in the Americas"; Grady, "Death at the Corners"; Sternberg, "Science, Legwork Combine to Catch Deadly Virus."

Chapter 7

Page 26: Butler's, Duchin's, and Moolenaar's activities described: Pendergrast, *Inside the Outbreaks*, 284–285.

Chapter 8

Page 28: Detection of hantavirus by CDC's VSPB and their subsequent activities described: Peters and Olshaker, *Virus Hunter: Thirty Years of Battling Hot Viruses Around the World*, 27–36.

Page 29: Hantavirus and its role in the founding of the EIS described: McKenna, *Beating Back the Devil: On the Front Lines with the Disease Detectives of the Epidemic Intelligence Service*, 10–18.

Page 29: As many as . . . died: Peters and Olshaker, *Virus Hunter*, 30.

Page 29: decided that the . . . service: Langmuir, "The Epidemic Intelligence Service of the Center for Disease Control," 472.

Page 29: He believed that . . . outbreaks: Henderson and Preston, *Smallpox: The Death of a Disease*, 23.

Page 30: The United States . . . troops: *Forensic Files*, season 4, episode 12, "With Every Breath," aired December 22, 1999.

Chapter 9

Page 31: "At that point . . . exposed.": Dr. James Cheek, interview with the author, August 23, 2022.

Page 32: "the story had . . . clicked.": Ibid.

Page 33: "When you're doing . . . from.": Ibid.

Chapter 10

Page 35: VSPB confirms TMI caused by different type of hantavirus: Peters and Olshaker, *Virus Hunter*, 34.

Chapter 11

Page 36: Rick Goodman's hantavirus cold case described: Peters and Olshaker, *Virus Hunter*, 36.

Chapter 12

Page 38: Rodent-trapping processes and relevant safety procedures described: Butler and Childs, "Of Mice and Men: Discovering a Deadly Hantavirus in the Americas"; Jamie Childs, interview with the author, July 7, 2022; Grady, "Death at the Corners"; Sternberg, "Tracking a Mysterious Killer Virus in the Southwest."

Page 40: "The bad news . . . in the United States.": Butler and Childs, "Of Mice and Men: Discovering a Deadly Hantavirus in the Americas."

Page 40: *Peromyscus maniculatus* distribution: Bunker, "*Peroymyscus maniculatus*."

Page 41: thirty-one people: Sternberg, "Rodent Virus Attack Not as Severe in '98."

Page 41: eleven died: Centers for Disease Control and Prevention,

"Outbreak of Hantavirus Infection—Southwestern United States, 1993."

Chapter 13

Page 42: there have been . . . US: Centers for Disease Control and Prevention, "Reported Cases of Hantavirus Disease."

PART II: JOHN SNOW AND THE MYSTERY OF THE BLUE DEATH

Chapter 14

Page 48: The first sign of . . . death: Mayo Clinic Staff, "Cholera."

Page 48: Seventh cholera pandemic: World Health Organization, "Cholera: Global Situation," 2023.

Page 49: "The pit is one huge privy . . . unwashed hands.": Snow, *On the Mode of Communication of Cholera*, 20.

Page 50: "It is amongst . . . introduced.": Snow, *On the Mode and Communication of Cholera*, 20.

Page 50: "the better . . . another.": Ibid.

Chapter 15

Page 51: London was . . . miles: Johnson, *The Ghost Map*, 12.

Page 52: 1850s London's sanitation problems: Ibid., 27–28.

Page 52: Night soil men's activities described: Ibid., 8–10.

Page 53: Cesspool cellars described: Ibid., 10.

Page 53: Snow describes his cholera theory: Snow, *On the Mode of Communication of Cholera*, 10.

Page 53: Snow describes his suspicions of the Broad Street water pump: Ibid., 38, 39.

Chapter 16

Page 55: John Snow describes his investigation into the Golden Square outbreak: Snow, *On the Mode of Communication of Cholera*, 42.

Page 55: Victorian workhouses described: Higginbotham, "The Workhouse: The Story of an Institution . . ."; Johnson, *The Ghost Map*, 265–266; Brain, "The Victorian Workhouse."

Page 57: The evolution and significance of Snow's maps and methods of investigation described: Johnson, *The Ghost Map*, 193–199; Vinten-Johansen, *Cholera, Chloroform, and the Science of Medicine: A Life of John Snow*, 395–396.

Chapter 17

Page 60: "an attack of . . . death.": Baby Lewis death record quoted in Johnson, *The Ghost Map*, 178–179.

Page 61: more than 600 . . . weeks: Ibid., 161.

Chapter 18

Page 63: the WHO . . . annually: World Health Organization, "Cholera: Global Situation," 2022.

Page 64: Filippo Pacini's early cholera work described: Johnson, *The Ghost Map*, 98–99; Frerichs, "Who First Discovered *Vibrio cholera*?"

PART III: THE HUNT FOR THE 1918 FLU

Chapter 19

Page 69: Roscoe Vaughan's course of illness described: Kolata, *Flu: The Story of the Great Influenza Pandemic of 1918 and the Search for the Virus That Caused It*, ch. 1.

Page 70: The day that . . . symptoms: Byerly, "The Influenza Pandemic of 1918–1919."

Page 70: "Opinion: influenza.": Sternberg, "A Doughboy's Lungs Yield 1918 Flu Virus."

Page 70: 56,000 troops: Robbins, "The First Wave: Remembering the Influenza Pandemic of 1918–19."

Page 70: Within a month . . . ill: Durr, "Flu Outbreak Killed 45,000 U.S. Soldiers during World War I."

Page 72: The So-Called Spanish Flu: Sowards, "How the 1918 Spanish Flu Pandemic Links to World War I."

Page 73: "Within a few months . . . planet.": McMillen, *Pandemics: A Very Short Introduction*, 90.

Page 73: 675,000 people died . . . alone: Centers for Disease Control and Prevention, "The 1918 Flu Pandemic: Why It Matters 100 Years Later"; Sturner, "1918 Flu & COVID-19: A Tale of Two Pandemics."

Page 73: In India . . . people perished: Biswas, "Coronavirus: What India Can Learn from the Deadly 1918 Flu."

Page 74: "was as much . . . populations.": McMillen, *Pandemics: A Very Short Introduction*, 91.

Page 74: In China . . . 100 million: Ibid., 90, 91.

Page 75: Discrimination against Black female nurses by the Army Nursing Corps described: O'Gan, "Victory at Home and Abroad."

Page 76: Not everyone agreed . . . sentence: Hauser, "The Mask Slackers of 1918."

Page 76: "some of the . . . riding.": Crosby, *America's Forgotten Pandemic*, ch. 7.

Page 76: Many people opposed . . . the coronavirus: Andrejko et al., "Effectiveness of Face Mask or Respirator Use in Indoor Public

Settings . . ."; Centers for Disease Control and Prevention, "CDC calls on Americans to Wear Masks to Prevent COVID-19 Spread."

Chapter 20

Page 78: The Hultins' travels with Otto Geist described: Kolata, *Flu: The Story of the Great Influenza Pandemic of 1918 and the Search for the Virus That Caused It*, ch. 4.

Page 78: In the 1920s . . . crew: Skarland, "Otto William Geist, 1888–1963."

Chapter 21

Page 80: The genesis of Hultin's idea to search for the 1918 influenza with the help of Otto Geist described: Kolata, *Flu*, ch. 4.

Chapter 22

Page 82: The 1918 flu had . . . virus: Kolata, *Flu*, ch. 4

Page 83: Hultin's flight to Alaska: Davies, *Catching Cold*, 235.

Page 84: Hultin gathered . . . warmth: Laden, *We Heard the Bells*.

Page 84: The mass grave . . . buried.: Kolata, *Flu*, ch. 4.

Page 84: "Fortunately for me . . . alive.": Johan Hultin interviewed in Laden, *We Heard the Bells*.

Page 84: "If you allow . . . vaccine.": Ibid.

Page 85: Excavation of the mass grave described: Kolata, *Flu*, ch. 4.

Page 85: and discovered three . . . bodies: Johan Hultin interviewed in Laden, *We Heard the Bells*.

Page 86: "there were no . . . catastrophe.": Kolata, *Flu*, ch. 4.

Page 86: Safety measures taken during the excavation of the mass grave described: Ibid.

Page 86: "We should have . . . again.": Johan Hultin quoted in Kolata, *Flu*, ch. 4.

Page 86: "I remembered . . . form.": Ibid.

Chapter 23

Page 88: Hultin and Whitney's processing of tissue and the attempt to grow the 1918 virus in chicken eggs described: Kolata, *Flu*, ch. 4.

Page 89: History and process of using eggs in vaccine production described: Centers for Disease Control and Prevention, "How Flu Vaccines Are Made"; Yeung, "The US keeps millions of chickens in secret farms to make flu vaccines. But their eggs won't work for coronavirus."

Page 89: He next attempted . . . as well: Roberts, "Facts and Ideas from Anywhere."

Page 89: "Week after week . . . window.": Johan Hultin quoted in Laden, *We Heard the Bells.*

Page 89: within six weeks . . . left: Davies, *Catching Cold*, 236.

Chapter 24

Page 91: Taubenberger's childhood described: Kolata, *Flu*, ch. 7.

Page 92: Taubenberger's discovery of the John Dalton eyeball experiment described: Ibid.

Page 92: "Clever . . . medicine.": Taubenberger, "Sanger Series: 'Going Viral' Featuring Jeffery K. Taubenberger."

Page 92: Taubenberger's decision to pursue the study of 1918 flu described: Kolata, *Flu*, ch. 7.

Page 93: "understat[ed] the total . . . half." Crosby, *America's Forgotten Pandemic*, ch. 26.

Page 93: "A pandemic of . . . again.": Taubenberger, "Why Study the 1918 Influenza Pandemic?"

Chapter 25

Page 95: "Chances of success . . . remote.": Conversations with Pathologists: Jeffery Taubenberger.

Page 96: The eighty-seven-year-old samples arrived . . . reports: Larson, "The Flu Hunters."

Page 96: Taubenberger and Reid's narrowing of their research criteria described: National Museum of Health and Medicine. "Closing in on a Killer: Scientists Unlock Clues to the Spanish Influenza Virus"; see also: Morens, Taubenberger, and Fauci, "Predominant Role of Bacterial Pneumonia as a Cause of Death in Pandemic Influenza"; Larson, "The Flu Hunters."

Chapter 26

Page 97: barely the width of a red blood cell: Racaniello, "This Week in Virology: 1918 Influenza with Jeffery Taubenberger."

Page 98: fragments of . . . them: Sternberg, "A Doughboy's Lungs Yield 1918 Flu Virus," 172.

Page 98: The role of hemagglutinin and neuraminidase in influenza viruses described: Desai, "Naming the Flu: H-Something, N-Something."

Page 98: Taubenberger describes the 1918 influenza's possible origins in birds and pigs: Racaniello, "This Week in Virology: 1918 Influenza with Jeffery Taubenberger."

Page 99: "Since 1918 . . . virus.": Taubenberger, "Sanger Series: 'Going Viral' Featuring Jeffery K. Taubenberger."

Page 99: "It's not just . . . humans.": Racaniello, "This Week in Virology: 1918 Influenza with Jeffery Taubenberger."

Chapter 27

Page 100: Johan Hultin describes reading about Dr. Taubenberger's work and their resulting partnership: Laden, *We Heard the Bells*.

Page 100: "This is not just a . . . outbreaks.": Taubenberger quoted in Sternberg, "A Doughboy's Lungs Yield 1918 Flu Virus," 172.

Chapter 28

Page 102: Hultin's August 1997 trip to Alaska and excavation of the mass grave in Brevig described: Davies, *Catching Cold*, 238–240; Laden, *We Heard the Bells*.

Page 103: at the age of . . . skis: McKnight, "Into the Wild. Twice. For Mankind."

Page 103: "The right man . . . time.": Eileen Hultin quoted in Davies, *Catching Cold*, 237.

Page 103: Hultin's exhumation of the Iñupiaq woman's body described: Laden, *We Heard the Bells*; Kolata, *Flu*, ch. 9.

Chapter 29

Page 106: Taubenberger describes the approval process and security measures involved in the revivification of the 1918 influenza virus: Taubenberger, "Sanger Series: 'Going Viral' Featuring Jeffery K. Taubenberger."

Page 108: Safety procedures within BSL-3 labs described: Roos, "NIH Panel Supports Stronger Safeguards for H5N1 Research."

Page 109: Dr. Terrence Tumpey explains how and why he revived the 1918 influenza: Honigsbaum, "Resurrecting the Killer."

Page 109: Tumpey's work with the 1918 influenza virus and subsequent results described: Tumpey et al., "Characterization of the Reconstructed 1918 Spanish Influenza Pandemic Virus"; Centers for Disease Control, "Flu Fighter: Terrence Tumpey Ph.D."; Honigsbaum, "Resurrecting the Killer"; Tumpey, "Genetically Engineering the Avian Flu."

Page 110: "All of the sudden . . . lethal.": Tumpey, "Genetically Engineering the Avian Flu."

Chapter 30

Page 111: Cytokine storm basics and its possible role in 1918 pandemic deaths: Pfizer, "Inside a Cytokine Storm: When Your Immune System Is Too Strong"; Robson, "Why the Flu of 1918 Was so Deadly."

Page 113: Seasonal flu statistics and vaccine benefits: Centers for Disease Control and Prevention, "Vaccine Effectiveness: How Well Do Flu Vaccines Work"; Mayo Clinic Staff, "Flu Shot: Your Best Bet for Avoiding Influenza."

PART IV: THE SMALLPOX HUNTERS

Chapter 31

Page 117: Neil Vora's cowpox investigation in the country of Georgia described: Vora et al., "Human Infection with a Zoonotic Orthopoxvirus in the Country of Georgia."

Page 118: Anthrax basics: Centers for Disease Control and Prevention, "What Is Anthrax?"

Page 119: "He survived . . . today.": Neil Vora, interview with the author, September 2, 2022.

Page 119: Neil Vora's family and career: Ibid.

Chapter 32

Page 121: During the twentieth . . . smallpox: American Museum of Natural History, "Online Exhibition: Smallpox."

Chapter 33

Page 123: Smallpox is believed . . . communities: Henderson and Preston, *Smallpox: The Death of a Disease*, 36.

Page 123: "after seeing . . . poxvirus.": Hopkins, "Ramses V: Earliest Known Victim?", 22.

Page 124: Plague of Athens statistics from abstract: Littman, "The Plague of Athens: Epidemiology and Paleopathology."

Page 124: "The exterior of . . . linens.": Mark, "Thucydides on the Plague of Athens: Text and Commentary."

Page 124: In the sixth . . . people: Centers for Disease Control and Prevention, "History of Smallpox."

Page 125: Jenner's development of the first vaccine described: Centers for Disease Control and Prevention, "History of Smallpox."

Page 126: 400,000 people . . . monarchs: Riedel, "Edward Jenner and the History of Smallpox and Vaccination."

Chapter 34

Page 128: Smallpox incubation period: Centers for Disease Control and Prevention, "Smallpox: Clinical Disease."

Page 128: Incubation period of smallpox in Lincoln's body: Foege, *House on Fire*, 7.

Page 128: Historical accounts . . . money: Basler, "Did President Lincoln Give the Smallpox to William H. Johnson?"

Page 128: "never hesitated.": Ibid.

Page 128: Historians believe . . . illness: Rosenwald, "Suffering from Smallpox after Gettysburg, Lincoln May Have Infected His Valet."

Page 128: Modes of smallpox transmission described: Centers for

Disease Control and Prevention, "Transmission: How Does Smallpox Spread?"

Chapter 35

Page 131: The assembly welcomed . . . worldwide: Henderson and Preston, *Smallpox: The Death of a Disease*, 61.

Page 131: Under the WHO's . . . immunity: Ibid., 62, 89.

Page 131: However, by the mid-1960s . . . available: World Health Organization, "The Global Eradication of Smallpox: Final Report of the Global Commission for the Certification of Smallpox Eradication"; Breman, "Donald Ainslie Henderson (1928–2016)."

Page 132: The American agency . . . campaigns: Centers for Disease Control and Prevention, "Smallpox Eradication."

Chapter 36

Page 134: 12 million . . . world: Foege, *House on Fire*, 44, 46.

Page 135: Foege and Thompson's trip to Ovirpua described: Ibid., 54–58.

Page 136: Foege radioed . . . cases of smallpox: Ibid., 57.

Page 137: "First we vaccinated . . . difficult.": Ibid.

Page 138: "If a house . . . eradicating smallpox.": Ibid., epigraph.

Page 139: half a billion people: Brilliant, *Sometimes Brilliant*, ch. 17.

Chapter 37

Page 140: Twenty million babies . . . vaccinated: Brilliant, *Sometimes Brilliant*, ch. 10.

Page 140: 150,000 virus hunters: Brilliant, *Sometimes Brilliant*, ch. 10.

Page 141: One week per . . . house calls: Ibid.

Page 141: half a million . . . homes.: Brilliant, *Sometimes Brilliant*, ch. 9.

Page 141: the number of . . . shots: Brilliant, *Sometimes Brilliant*, ch. 10.

Page 141: It's estimated that . . . paperwork: Lalla and Boissière, "Smallpox Eradication in India, 1972–1977."

Page 141: Search teams' other monthly surveillance activities described: Brilliant, *Sometimes Brilliant*, ch. 10; Lalla and Boissière, "Smallpox Eradication in India, 1972–1977."

Page 142: By 1973 . . . free: World Health Organization, "The Global Eradication of Smallpox: Final Report of the Global Commission for the Certification of Smallpox Eradication."

Chapter 38

Page 144: "I was captivated . . . world.": Guinan and Mather, *Adventures of a Female Medical Detective: In Pursuit of Smallpox and AIDS*, ch. 2.

Page 145: At the time . . . "distract the men.": Ibid.

Page 145: Mary Guinan's early science career: Ibid.

Page 147: "Our job was . . . immunity.": Ibid.

Page 147: Guinan's transportation problems in India: Ibid., ch. 3.

Page 148: "the elephant . . . team." . . . ahead of schedule.: Ibid.

Chapter 39

Page 150: Dr. Davis's discovery of possible smallpox cases in Bangladesh described: Dr. Connie Davis, interview with the author, September 11, 2023.

Page 151: "but once I . . . focused.": Davis, *Searching for Sitala Mata: Eradicating Smallpox in India*, ch. 15.

Page 151: where no . . . May 24: Lalla and Boissière, "Smallpox Eradication in India, 1972–1977."

Page 151: "I could just . . . *American*.": Davis, *Searching for Sitala Mata*, ch. 15.

Page 153: "Willingness to serve . . . emergency.": GirlScouts.org, "Traditions and Ceremonies."

Page 153: "An older man . . . smallpox.": Davis, *Searching for Sitala Mata*, ch. 16.

Page 155: Davis was eventually . . . months: Ganneri, "These Memoirs Show Us the Role Women Had in Eradicating Smallpox from India."

Page 155: After July 5 . . . country: Lalla and Boissière, "Smallpox Eradication in India, 1972–1977."

Chapter 40

Page 158: "People rarely reflect . . . past.": Foege, *House on Fire*, epigraph.

Page 158: Mpox statistics updated by CDC: Centers for Disease Control and Prevention, "2022–2023 Mpox Outbreak Global Map"; World Health Organization, "Multi-Country Outbreak of Mpox: External Situation Report #27."

Page 159: "The [mpox] situation . . . vaccine.": Neil Vora, interview with the author, September 2, 2022.

Page 159: "Infectious diseases . . . for.": Ibid.

Page 159: The eradication of . . . infection: Wayne and Bolker, *Infectious Disease: A Very Short Introduction*, 1, 4.

PART V: HIV/AIDS: A CASE OF MEDICAL ACTIVISM IN AMERICA

Chapter 41

Page 164: "top priority.": Weinraub, "Reagan Hears AIDS Has No. 1 Priority."

Page 164: By the summer . . . died: National Library of Medicine, "Reports of the Surgeon General: The AIDS Epidemic."

Page 165: A person died . . . minutes: *United in Anger: A History of ACT UP*, Jim Hubbard, dir.

Page 165: By the end of 1990, there . . . deaths: The Foundation for AIDS Research (amfAR), "Snapshots of an Epidemic: An HIV/AIDS Timeline."

Page 166: "Dr. Anthony Fauci . . . Diseases.": Garance Franke-Ruta interviewed in *How to Survive a Plague*, David France, dir.

Page 166: "We want them to . . . disease.": Garance Franke-Ruta interviewed in *United in Anger: A History of ACT UP*, Jim Hubbard, dir.

Page 167: Sixty-five percent . . . AIDS: Colangelo, ed. "We Are Everywhere: Lesbians in the Archive."

Page 167: "the third leading . . . group.": Pellowski, Kalichman, Matthews, and Adler, "A Pandemic of the Poor: Social Disadvantage and the U.S. HIV Epidemic," 3.

Page 168: "I'm fine . . . Tony?": Staley, "Anthony Fauci Quietly Shocked Us All."

Chapter 42

Page 169: HIV impacts on the human body described: Nall, "How Does HIV Affect the Body?"

Page 170: Peter Staley's life, career, and activism: Peter Staley, interview with the author, December 4, 2023.

Chapter 43

Page 172: "Being a busy young . . . away." Anthony Fauci interviewed in *Fauci*, John Hoffman and Janet Tobias, dirs.

Page 173: Fauci's vasculitis discovery described: Davies, "Long Before COVID-19, Dr. Anthony Fauci 'Changed Medicine in America Forever'"; Anthony Fauci, interview by Victoria Harden, "In Their Own Words . . . NIH Researchers Recall the Early Years of AIDS," 1989.

Page 174: Vasculitis death rate: Harden, *AIDS at 30: A History*, ch. 3.

Page 174: It was a . . . customers: Anthony Fauci, interview by Peter Staley, "A Conversation with Dr. Anthony Fauci, October 26, 2022."

Page 174: Tony was named . . . squad: Borrell, *The First Shots: The Epic Rivalries and Heroic Science Behind the Race to the Coronavirus Vaccine*.

Page 174: "It's what drove . . . school.": Anthony Fauci interviewed in *Fauci*, John Hoffman and Janet Tobias, dirs.

Page 175: *Oh my God* . . . "goosebumps.": Ibid.

Page 175: "Some people . . . me.": Anthony Fauci quoted in Harden, *AIDS at 30: A History*, ch. 3.

Page 175: "But the fact . . . yet.": Ibid.

Page 175: "It was clear . . . problem.": Anthony Fauci, interview by Victoria Harden, "In Their Own Words . . . NIH Researchers Recall the Early Years of AIDS," 1993.

Page 175: "it wasn't restricted . . . men.": Anthony Fauci, interview by Janet Heininger, "Edward M. Kennedy Oral History Project."

Page 176: "I wanted to . . . was.": Anthony Fauci, interview by Victoria Harden, "In Their Own Words . . . NIH Researchers Recall the Early Years of AIDS," 1989.

Page 176: "Every once in . . . bad."; "It was just . . . anything.": Anthony Fauci interviewed in *Fauci*, John Hoffman and Janet Tobias, dirs.

Chapter 44

Page 177: "A Working Confrontation": France, dir., *How to Survive a Plague*.

Page 177: "I decided that I would be . . . doing.": Anthony Fauci, interview by Peter Staley, "A Conversation with Dr. Anthony Fauci."

Page 178: "was the first . . . us.": Peter Staley interviewed in *How to Survive a Plague*, David France, dir.

Page 178: "The criticism . . . him.": David Barr quoted in *Fauci*, John Hoffman and Janet Tobias, dirs.

Page 178: "He got a . . . conversation.": Peter Staley quoted in *Fauci*, John Hoffman and Janet Tobias, dirs.

Page 178: "I couldn't shake . . . hands.": Staley, "Anthony Fauci Quietly Shocked Us All."

Page 179: "[The activists] elevated . . . about.": Anthony Fauci quoted in *How to Survive a Plague*, David France, dir.

Page 179: "agree on everything . . . right.": Anthony Fauci quoted in *Fauci*, John Hoffman and Janet Tobias, dirs.

Page 179: "The way we . . . needed.": Anthony Fauci, interview by Victoria Harden, "In Their Own Words . . .", 1993.

Page 179: "You cannot just . . . population.": Ibid.

Page 179: Fauci describes his work to unite the activist and scientific communities: Ibid.

Chapter 45

Page 181: "On Monday nights . . . for them" . . . in attendance.: Jim Eigo, interview by Sarah Schulman, "ACT UP Oral History Project."

Page 182: When a member was . . . person: Sarah Schulman, email message to author, June 1, 2023.

Page 182: "a twelve-ring . . . moments.": Staley, *Never Silent: ACT UP and My Life in Activism*, ch. 7.

Page 182: "The latest science . . . level.": Ibid.

Chapter 46

Page 184: The list of demands that ACT UP presented to FDA commissioner Frank Young described: *How to Survive a Plague*, David France, dir.

Page 185: "appear[ed] safe and . . . effective.": Leary, "FDA Pressed to Approve More AIDS Drugs."

Page 185: "I'm here today . . . quicker.": Vito Russo quoted in *United in Anger: A History of ACT UP*, Jim Hubbard, dir.

Page 186: "Go find someone . . . locally.": Ann Northrop quoted in Sharfstein, "1988 AIDS Protest at the FDA."

Page 186: "We made the . . . Washington, DC.": Mark Harrington quoted in Sharfstein, *The Public Health Crisis Survival Guide: Leadership and Management in Trying Times*, 171.

Page 187: "ACT UP's big, national . . . out.": Staley, *Never Silent*, ch. 8.

Page 187: The national AIDS . . . begun.: *United in Anger: A History of ACT UP*, Jim Hubbard, dir.

Chapter 47

Page 188: An antiviral medication . . . patients: Buhles, "Compassionate Use: A Story of Ethics and Science in the Development of a New Drug," 304.

Page 189: Doctors who prescribed . . . CMV: Ibid., 308.

Page 189: Syntex and the ganciclovir controversy and aftermath described: Sharfstein, *The Public Health Crisis Survival Guide: Leadership and Management in Trying Times*, 172–175; Buhles, "Compassionate Use: A Story of Ethics and Science in the Development of a New Drug," 304–314.

Page 190: One called the . . . "mean.": Kolata, "FDA Said to Be Re-Evaluating Order for More Studies on an AIDS Drug."

Page 190: "Who's there . . . blind.": Anthony Fauci quoted in *Fauci*, John Hoffman and Janet Tobias, dirs.

Page 190: "I think it's . . . medically.": Anthony Fauci quoted in Kolata, "FDA Approves the Use of an Experimental Drug for AIDS Patients' Eye Infections."

Page 190: It was a . . . well: Ibid.

Page 191: "Under pressure . . . drug.": Ibid.

Page 191: Ganciclovir still the preferred first-line treatment for cytomegalovirus: HIV.gov Clinical Info, "Guidelines for the Prevention and Treatment of Opportunistic Infections in Adults and Adolescents with HIV."

Chapter 48

Page 192: "People of color . . . excluded.": Mark Harrington quoted in Sharfstein, *The Public Health Crisis Survival Guide: Leadership and Management in Trying Times*, 175.

Page 193: Parallel track procedures described: Ibid., 177.

Page 193: "on a case-by-case basis.": Frank Young quoted in Kolata, "AIDS Researcher Seeks Wide Access to Drugs in Tests."

Chapter 49

Page 195: "HIV infection was . . . death.": Centers for Disease Control and Prevention, "Mortality Attributable to HIV Infection/AIDS Among Persons Aged 25–44 Years—United States, 1990, 1991."

Page 195: 160,000 Americans . . . War: The Foundation for AIDS Research (amfAR), "Snapshots of an Epidemic: An HIV/AIDS Timeline."

Page 195: "We didn't have . . . game.": Staley, *Never Silent: ACT UP and My Life in Activism*, ch. 9.

Page X: Protests taking place outside the Moscone Center described: CBS News Staff, "Activists Look Back at Anniversary of Historic San Francisco ACT UP Protests."

Page 196: "There were lines of . . . gear.": Staley, *Never Silent: ACT UP and My Life in Activism*, ch. 9.

Page 197: "promote, encourage . . . activities.": S.Amdt.963 to H.R.3058, 100th Congress (1987–1988).

Page 197: "I'd like to . . . GEORGE?": Peter Staley quoted in archival footage, *How to Survive a Plague*, David France, dir.

Page 198: thousands took the cue . . . conference: Concar, "Protests Oust Science at AIDS Conference."

Page 198: "You can all . . . ACT UP.": Staley, "Peter Staley Speech at the Sixth International Conference on AIDS."

Page 198: "We hadn't burned . . . over.": Staley, *Never Silent: ACT UP and My Life in Activism*, ch. 9.

Page 198: "I have always . . . us?": Staley, "Peter Staley Speech at the Sixth International Conference on AIDS."

Page 198: "Scientists . . . are confronted . . . goal.": Fauci, "Anthony Fauci Speech at the Sixth International AIDS Conference."

Page 199: "including employment . . . services.": US Department of Labor, "Americans with Disabilities Act."

Page 199: improve the quality . . . HIV: HRSA: Ryan White HIV/AIDS Program, "Thirty Years of Innovating Care, Optimizing Public Health, Ending the HIV Epidemic."

Page 199: While President Bush . . . US Congress: Urvashi Vaid, interview by Ailsa Chang, "Critics of President George H. W. Bush Reflect on His Handling of the AIDS Crisis."

Page 200: "We had finally . . . table.": Staley, *Never Silent: ACT UP and My Life in Activism*, ch. 9.

Chapter 50

Page 201: 10 million people . . . HIV: The Foundation for AIDS Research (amfAR), "Snapshots of an Epidemic: An HIV/AIDS Timeline."

Page 201: The following year . . . 44: HIV.gov, "A Timeline of HIV and AIDS."

Page 201: By 1994 . . . group: Ibid.

Page 201: "It was a . . . time.": David Barr quoted in *How to Survive a Plague*, David France, dir.

Page 201: How AZT works: Thaczuk, "AZT (Zidovudine, Retrovir)."

Page 202: "we got lucky.": David Barr quoted in *How to Survive a Plague*, David France, dir.

Page 202: How protease inhibitors fight HIV infection: Mudgal, Birudukota, and Doke, "Applications of Click Chemistry in the Development of HIV Protease Inhibitors," 1.

Page 202: Six months . . . HIV/AIDS: HRSA: Ryan White HIV/AIDS Program, "First Protease Inhibitor Becomes Available."

Chapter 51

Page 203: "We were calling . . . medicine.": Anthony Fauci quoted in McMurry, "The Elephant in the Room: What about HIV?"

Page 203: "One by one" . . . 1996.: Staley, *Never Silent: ACT UP and My Life in Activism*, ch. 12.

Page 204: "When future generations . . . free.": Russo, *Why We Fight*.

Page 205: 99 percent effective . . . infection: Krellenstein, Lord, and Staley, "Why Don't More Americans Use PrEP?"

Page 205: five HIV-positive . . . diagnosis: Highleyman, "First Person May Be Cured of HIV after Stem Cell Transplant without CCR5 Mutation."

Page 205: In the US . . . year: Office of Disease Prevention and Health Promotion, "HIV Workgroup."

Page 205: At the end . . . HIV: Centers for Disease Control and Prevention, "HIV Basics."

Page 206: "I went from . . . involved.": Anthony Fauci quoted in McMurry, "The Elephant in the Room: What about HIV?"

Page 206: Origin story of the Vaccine Research Center: Kolata and Mueller, "Halting Progress and Happy Accidents: How mRNA Vaccines Were Made."

PART VI: COVID-19 AND THE VACCINE HUNTERS

Chapter 52

Page 212: Karikó's childhood behind the Iron Curtain and her departure from Hungary described: Johnson, "A One-Way Ticket. A Cash-Stuffed Teddy Bear. A Dream Decades in the Making."; Zuckerman, *A Shot to Save the World: The Inside Story of the Life-or-Death Race for a Covid-19 Vaccine*, ch. 5.

Page 212: "software of life.": Moderna, Inc., "United States Securities and Exchange Commission, Form 10-K."

Page 212: Karikó's introduction to, and fascination with, mRNA described: Cox, "How mRNA Went from a Scientific Backwater to a Pandemic Crusher."

Page 212: mRNA's role in immunity: Moderna, "The Power of mRNA."

Page 213: While it was possible . . . exist.: Cox, "How mRNA Went from a Scientific Backwater to a Pandemic Crusher."

Page 213: Kariko's struggles with laboratory funding described: Park and Ducharme, "The Miracle Workers."

Page 213: "I never wanted to . . . leave.": Nair, "QnAs with Katalin Karikó."

Page 213: The communist government . . . $100: Ibid.

Chapter 53

Page 215: Descriptions of mRNA . . . with: Johnson, "A One-Way Ticket. A Cash-Stuffed Teddy Bear. A Dream Decades in the Making."

Page 216: Karikó's struggle to fit in at the University of Pennsylvania described: Zuckerman, *A Shot to Save the World*, ch. 5.

Page 216: Katalin's boss intervened . . . "disruptive.": Ibid.

Page 216: Karikó's struggles to fund her experiments and her subsequent demotion at the University of Pennsylvania described: Park and Ducharme, "The Miracle Workers."

Page 217: "I thought of . . . experiments.": Katalin Karikó quoted in Garde and Saltzman, "The Story of mRNA: How a Once-Dismissed Idea Became a Leading Technology in the COVID Vaccine Race."

Chapter 54

Page 218: Karikó and Weissman's first meeting described: Yu, "How Scientists Drew Weissman (MED'87, GRS'87) and Katalin Karikó Developed the Revolutionary mRNA Technology inside COVID Vaccines"; Cox, "How mRNA Went from a Scientific Backwater to a Pandemic Crusher"; Hoyle, "Honoring mRNA Pioneers Katalin Karikó and Drew Weissman | 20-Minute Health Talk."

Page 219: Weissman's background described: Kolata and Mueller, "Halting Progress and Happy Accidents: How mRNA Vaccines Were Made."; Zuckerman, *A Shot to Save the World*, ch. 5.

Page 219: "I am an . . . mRNA.": Katalin Karikó quoted in Kolata and Mueller, "Halting Progress and Happy Accidents: How mRNA Vaccines Were Made."

Page 220: "Their fur got . . . why.": Drew Weissman quoted in ibid.

Page 221: "We were both . . . results.": Drew Weissman quoted in Karikó and Weissman, "The Story Behind mRNA Covid Vaccines."

Page 221: Discovery of uses of uridine and pseudouridine described: Zuckerman, *A Shot to Save the World*, ch. 5; Nair, "QnAs with Katalin Karikó."

Page 221: "We realized at" . . . therapy.: Drew Weissman quoted in Cox, "How mRNA Went from a Scientific Backwater to a Pandemic Crusher."

Page 222: "Nobody invited us . . . nothing.": Katalin Karikó quoted in ibid.

Chapter 55

Page 223: Eight days earlier . . . samples: Holmes, "Eddie Holmes: De-Coding COVID-19."

Page 224: Zhang's discovery of the coronavirus and the release of its genome sequence described: Zuckerman, *A Shot to Save the World*, ch. 14.

Page 224: a new coronavirus . . . Asia: Centers for Disease Control and Prevention, "CDC SARS Response Timeline."

Page 224: Symptoms began . . . countries: World Health Organization, "Severe Acute Respiratory Syndrome (SARS)."

Page 224: infecting 8,098 . . . 774: Centers for Disease Control and Prevention, "Frequently Asked Questions about SARS."

Page 224: eight people . . . fatalities: Ibid.

Page 224: Masked palm civet's connection to SARS pandemic: Centers for Disease Control and Prevention, "Notice of Embargo of Civets."

Page 225: They closed the . . . reported: Worobey et al., "The Huanan

Seafood Wholesale Market in Wuhan Was the Early Epicenter of the COVID-19 Pandemic."

Page 226: Zhang and Holmes's publicizing of the coronavirus sequence: Zuckerman, *A Shot to Save the World*, ch. 14.

Page 226: "All, an initial . . . available.": Eddie Holmes (@edwardcholmes), Twitter, January 10, 2020, 8:08 p.m., twitter.com/edwardcholmes/status/1215802670176276482?lang=en.

Chapter 56

Page 229: 2012 MERS outbreak: Centers for Disease Control and Prevention, "Middle East Respiratory Syndrome (MERS)."

Page 229: As of this writing . . . SARS: Donnelly et al., "Worldwide Reduction in MERS Cases and Deaths Since 2016."

Page 230: Barney Graham and Jason McLellan's collaboration on MERS described: Park and Ducharme, "The Miracle Workers."

Chapter 57

Page 231: Graham, McLellan begin study of HKU1: Kramer, "They Spent 12 Years Solving a Puzzle. It Yielded the First COVID-19 Vaccines."

Page 232: Pre-fusion and post-fusion conformation of coronavirus spike described: Cross, "The Tiny Tweak Behind COVID-19 Vaccines"; Pallesen et al., "Immunogenicity and Structures of a Rationally Designed Prefusion MERS-CoV Spike Antigen."

Chapter 58

Page 234: a profession . . . men: Kozlowski et al., "Intersectional Inequalities in Science."

Page 234: Myrtis Bradsher . . . day.; "a class for exceptional students.": Fears, "Kizzmekia Corbett Spent Her Life Preparing for This Moment. Can She Create the Vaccine to End a Pandemic?"

Page 235: The first time . . . scientist: Corbett, "Preparing for a Pandemic: Dr. Kizzmekia Corbett."

Page 235: "Even though I . . . forever.": Corbett, "Kizzmekia Corbett: Scientist, Vaccine Developer, and Tar Heel."

Page 236: Kizzmekia Corbett's academic career described: Fears, "Kizzmekia Corbett Spent Her Life Preparing for This Moment. Can She Create the Vaccine to End a Pandemic?"

Page 236: "first-generation . . . college.": Corbett, "Kizzmekia Corbett: Scientist, Vaccine Developer, and Tar Heel."

Page 236: "I want your job.": Barney Graham quoted in Ross, "Meet Kizzmekia Corbett, the 34-Year-Old Scientist Developing a Vaccine for Coronavirus."

Chapter 59

Page 238: Rossi was so . . . Moderna: Garde and Saltzman, "The Story of mRNA: How a Once-Dismissed Idea Became a Leading Technology in the Covid Vaccine Race."

Page 239: How the VRC/Moderna COVID-19 vaccine works: Cross, "The Tiny Tweak Behind COVID-19 Vaccines"; Pallesen et al., "Immunogenicity and Structures of a Rationally Designed Prefusion MERS-CoV Spike Antigen"; Centers for Disease Control and Prevention, "Understanding How COVID-19 Vaccines Work."

Page 239: By the third week . . . "mRNA 1273.": Zuckerman, *A Shot to Save the World*, ch. 14.

Chapter 60

Page 241: "largest quarantine in world history": Markel, "Will the Largest Quarantine in History Just Make Things Worse?"; Levenson, "Scale of China's Wuhan Shutdown Is Believed to Be Without Precedent."

Page 241: "As of today . . . safety.": Alex Azar quoted in US Department of Health and Human Services, "Update on the New Coronavirus Outbreak First Identified in Wuhan, China."

Page 242: "We have already . . . outbreak.": Anthony Fauci quoted in ibid.

Page 242: Azar announces US declares that the new coronavirus is a public health emergency: NBC News, "Trump Administration Declares Coronavirus a Public Health Emergency."

Page 242: Two days later . . . outbreak: Reuters Staff, "China Coronavirus Deaths Rise 254 to 1,367 at End-Feb 12."

Page 242: "It's going to . . . disappear.": Summers, "Timeline: How Trump Has Downplayed the Coronavirus Pandemic."

Page 243: "In the past . . . hospitals.": Ghebreyesus, "Coronavirus Outbreak: WHO Declares COVID-19 a Global Pandemic."

Chapter 61

Page 245: Sixty-six days . . . trials: Corbett, et al., "SARS-CoV-2 mRNA Vaccine Design Enabled by Prototype Pathogen Preparedness," 568.

Page 245: what dose level . . . participants: Dr. Rituparna Das, interview with the author, December 14, 2022.

Page 245: Vaccine trial phases: Centers for Disease Control and Prevention, "How Vaccines Are Developed and Approved for Use."

Page 246: Jennifer Haller's participation in vaccine trials described: Simon, "'I Wanted to Do Something,' Says Mother of Two Who Is First to Test Coronavirus Vaccine."

Page 246: "I'm super proud . . . well.": Jennifer Haller quoted in *The Vaccine: Conquering COVID.*

Page 246: "I wanted to. . . given.": Jennifer Haller quoted in Simon, "'I Wanted to Do Something,' Says Mother of Two Who Is First to Test Coronavirus Vaccine."

Page 247: 2,583 incidents of racist language: Jeung et al., "Anti-Chinese Rhetoric Employed by Perpetrators of Anti-Asian Hate."

Page 247: And in 2020 . . . year: Center for the Study of Hate & Extremism (CSUSB), "Fact Sheet: Anti-Asian Prejudice March 2020."

Chapter 62

Page 248: BioNTech announces its mRNA vaccine: Pfizer, "Pfizer and BioNTech to Co-Develop Potential COVID-19 Vaccine."

Page 249: "BioNTech doesn't . . . website.": Katalin Karikó quoted in Cox, "How mRNA Went from a Scientific Backwater to a Pandemic Crusher."

Chapter 63

Page 250: "It's a recommendation . . . myself.": Donald Trump quoted in Tucker, Miller, and Schneider, "Face Coverings Recommended, but Trump Says He Won't Wear One."

Page 251: "The consequences could . . . appear.": Anthony Fauci quoted in Cancryn, "Fauci Warns Reopening Country Too Fast Could Be 'Really Serious' for States."

Page 251: Since mid-March . . . pandemic: Cohen, "Jobless Numbers Are 'Eye-Watering' but Understate the Crisis."

Page 251: half a million confirmed cases of COVID-19: Centers for Disease Control and Prevention, "CDC Museum COVID-19 Timeline."

Page 252: In Chicago . . . population.: Reyes, Husain, Gutowski, St. Clair, and Pratt, "Chicago's Coronavirus Disparity: Black Chicagoans Are Dying at Nearly Six Times the Rate of White Residents, Data Show."

Page 252: "nearly six times . . . residents.": Ibid.

Page 252: Among the hardest . . . families.: Ibid.

Page 252: Navajo Nation records highest rate of COVID-19 per capita in the U.S.: Centers for Disease Control and Prevention, "CDC Museum COVID-19 Timeline."

Chapter 64

Page 253: Federal government announces Operation Warp Speed program: Associated Press, "Trump Touts 'Operation Warp Speed' in Vaccine Hunt."

Page 253: Details of Operation Warp Speed described: *The Vaccine: Conquering COVID*; US Department of Health and Human Services, "Explaining Operation Warp Speed."

Page 254: PPE shortages: Burki, "Global Shortage of Personal Protective Equipment."

Page 255: Availability of vaccine for trial volunteers who received placebo: Rid, Lipsitch, and Miller, "The Ethics of Continuing Placebo in SARS-CoV-2 Vaccine Trials."

Chapter 65

Page 256: 75,000 new COVID-19 . . . day: Benner et al., "U.S. Reports More than 70,000 New Coronavirus Cases for the Second Time."

Page 256: More than 3 million Americans had the virus: AJMC Staff, "A Timeline of COVID-19 Developments in 2020."

Page 256: Dr. Fauci warned . . . 100,000.: Centers for Disease Control and Prevention, "CDC Museum COVID-19 Timeline."

Page 256: "We are not . . . communities.": Centers for Disease Control and Prevention, "CDC Calls on Americans to Wear Masks to Prevent COVID-19 Spread."

Page 257: 79 percent . . . white.: Borrell, *The First Shots*, ch. 21.; *The Vaccine: Conquering COVID*.

Page 257: The impact of health disparities on clinical trials: National Institute on Minority Health and Health Disparities, "Diversity and Inclusion in Clinical Trials"; Hall, "Health Equity Presentation, CDC Disease Detective Camp."

Page 257: By increasing . . . it: Cohen and Vigue, "COVID-19 Vaccine Trials Have Been Slow to Recruit Black and Latino People—and That Could Delay a Vaccine."

Page 258: Twice as many . . . study: *The Vaccine: Conquering COVID*.

Chapter 66

Page 259: Pfizer's Phase 3 vaccine trial results: *The Vaccine: Conquering COVID*; Pfizer, "Pfizer and BioNTech Announce Vaccine Candidate Against COVID-19 Achieved Success in First Interim Analysis from Phase 3 Study."

Page 260: "I didn't jump . . . story.": Katalin Karikó quoted in Cox, "How mRNA Went from a Scientific Backwater to a Pandemic Crusher."

Page 260: "I didn't celebrate . . . therapeutic.": Drew Weissman quoted in Karikó and Weissman, "The Story Behind mRNA COVID Vaccines."

Page 260: "There were a . . . had.": Drew Weissman quoted in Yu, "How Scientists Drew Weissman (MED'87, GRS'87) and Katalin Karikó Developed the Revolutionary mRNA Technology inside COVID Vaccines."

Page 260: "It was a lot . . . joy.": Katalin Karikó quoted in Karikó and Weissman, "The Story Behind mRNA COVID Vaccines."

Chapter 67

Page 262: "Well . . . say.": Kizzmekia Corbett quoted in Gale and Hellerman, *Race for the Vaccine: A CNN Film*.

Page 262: "There were ninety-five . . . [vaccine group]."; "which is even better news.": Barney Graham quoted in ibid.

Page 263: "I don't even . . . say.": Kizzmekia Corbett quoted in ibid.

Page 263: Operation Warp Speed vaccine distribution figures: Rummler, "U.S. Set to End 2020 with Just Over 3 Million Vaccine Doses Administered."

Chapter 68

Page 264: Sandra Lindsay . . . COVID-19: Tanner, "First COVID-19 Shot Recipient in US Now a Vaccine Activist"; Aubrey, "Sandra Lindsay Got the First U.S. COVID Jab. Here's Her Secret to Motivate Others."

Page 264: Globally, 2.3 billion . . . unvaccinated: Schellekens, "The Unfinished Business of COVID-19 Vaccination."

Page 266: "In general . . . mild.": World Health Organization, "COVID-19 Vaccines."

INDEX